Advance Praise for *Reckless Love*

"*Reckless Love* is short, sweet, and delightful. I love John Newton's stories—his Facebook story, to name one, is amazing!—and I love the way he tells them. Funny, mildly self-deprecatory, and entirely easy of access, they bring the book completely to life. And they are all in service of a disarmingly accessible intro to the core dynamics of Christian life: calm, compassion, total mercy, infectious humor, and honest joy. *Reckless Love* is a charming introduction to, well, the Good Lovin' (Young Rascals) of God."

—The Rev. Dr. Paul F. M. Zahl, retired dean and president
of Trinity Episcopal School for Ministry,
Ambridge, Pennsylvania

"John Newton bravely calls us to see the reckless love of Jesus with fresh eyes. He weaves his own witness with the relentless (and often offensive) message of the Gospel. I was left remembering that mercy for the sinner is the only real relief."

—The Rev. Sarah Condon, associate editor
of the *Mockingbird*, cohost of *The Mockingcast*, and Episcopal
priest at St. Martin's Church in Houston, Texas

"John Newton's *Reckless Love* clears away the cobwebs of fear, smallness, and perceptions of scarcity that seem to clutter the human condition with a wonderfully beautiful message—that we are deeply, profoundly, even 'recklessly' loved."

—The Rev. Marcus Halley, rector of St. Paul's Church on
Lake of the Isles in Minneapolis, Minnesota

"Our grace-starved world needs to hear good news. Thanks be to God for what John Newton has written, offering hopeful reflections on the ministry of Jesus and the witness of saints, sharing stories of transforming grace. The good news of God's reckless love described in this book offers a lens that can guide us forward with confidence and courage in a world marked by fake news. Each chapter, concluding with engaging questions, invites the reader into that way of seeing. You and your community will be blessed by taking this book to heart."

—The Rev. Jay Sidebotham, director of *RenewalWorks*

"John Newton reminds us that Jesus is with us in the broken places and Jesus is with us in our joy and celebration. On the floor in front of the church altar. At the bedside of a loved one where we keep watch. In the streets where we cry for justice. On the playground where laughter is carried on the wind. In the communities where we live. Jesus is here—and loves us . . . with love that is never-ending. With a love that is reckless."

—Roger Hutchison, author of *Jesus: God Among Us*

Reckless Love

The Scandal of Grace in a Performance-Driven World

John Newton

Church Publishing
NEW YORK

Church Publishing
19 East 34th Street
New York, NY 10016
www.churchpublishing.org

Cover design by Jennifer Kopec, 2Pug Design
Typeset by PerfecType, Nashville, Tennessee

Library of Congress Cataloging-in-Publication Data

Names: Newton, John (Canon), author.
Title: Reckless love : the scandal of grace in a performance-driven world /
    John Newton.
Description: New York : Church Publishing, 2018. | Includes index.
Identifiers: LCCN 2017053980 (print) | LCCN 2018010922 (ebook) | ISBN
    9781640650268 (ebook) | ISBN 9781640650251 (pbk.)
Subjects: LCSH: Bible. Gospels—Theology. | Episcopal Church—Doctrines. |
    Grace (Theology)
Classification: LCC BS2555.52 (ebook) | LCC BS2555.52 .N49 2018 (print) | DDC
    248.4/83—dc23
LC record available at https://lccn.loc.gov/2017053980

Printed in Canada

CONTENTS

INTRODUCTION: SIGHT

They came to Bethsaida. Some people brought a blind man to him and begged him to touch him. He took the blind man by the hand and led him out of the village; and when he had put saliva on his eyes and laid his hands on him, he asked him, "Can you see anything?" And the man looked up and said, "I can see people, but they look like trees, walking." Then Jesus laid his hands on his eyes again; and he looked intently and his sight was restored, and he saw everything clearly. (Mark 8:22–25)

There's an old joke about a man who visits the eye doctor. The receptionist asks the man the reason for his visit. The man complains, "I keep seeing spots in front of my eyes." The receptionist asks him, "Have you ever seen a doctor?" The man replies, "No, just spots."

This joke speaks to the question I want to frame for your reading this book: what do *you* see?

"Can you see anything?" Jesus asked the blind man from Bethsaida. Jesus asks us this same question. "Can you see anything good, beautiful, true, lasting, and holy amidst this performance-driven world of competition, violence, fear, impermanence, and greed?"

I recently noticed that a habit of mine was blurring my spiritual vision. Specifically, I imbibed the news on my iPhone the moment my alarm sounded. Before my feet touched the floor or my first sip of coffee, before I woke my daughter or kissed my wife or said my prayers, I began my day by reading a long list of things I need to fear. I then had an epiphany about the news itself, which I ask you to read with theological eyes and not political eyes: it is all *fake news*.

I don't mean that real facts aren't offered, that honest journalism doesn't exist, or that the news is devoid of integrity, because none of that is true. I mean that when reading the "news" was my morning habit, I began each day terrified. I feared our nation, other nations, and how our nation relates to other nations. I feared a terrorist attack, a cyberattack, a heart attack, and even a gluten attack. I don't even know what gluten is.

I began each day seeing, not what God sees, but what the market-driven media wanted me to see: namely, a world that is falling apart, a world where I have enemies that I need to protect myself and my children from, a world where my value, identity and performance are fused, and above all, a world that is *not* reconciled to God in Christ. Theologically speaking, *that* world is fake news, because Jesus Christ has been raised from the dead and Christ has gathered all of creation into God.

The "real news," from God's perspective, is always the surprising, hilarious, outrageously wonderful message that all of creation is restored in Christ *now*. One day we will see and experience the fullness of this restored creation. For now, Paul says, we see God's restored world only "in part" (see 1 Cor. 13:12). However, I know from experience that "in part" is better than "not at all" and that a small improvement in vision can yield miraculous results with respect to how we experience God, life, and even ourselves.

Thus, I begin each chapter in this book with a passage from one of the four Gospels—a piece of "real news," so to speak. Each chapter is intentionally brief and seeks to make visible the unrelenting love that God has for human beings. I did not write this book to tell you what you *should* be doing, but rather to help you see the reckless love of God in and through Jesus Christ.

A clearer vision of God's grace always breaks into our life when we least expect it. I experienced this firsthand recently when my car broke down. As the tow truck pulled up, all I saw was how much money the repairs would cost and how much time it would take to fix my car. Imagining those things made me feel lonely, sad, and apprehensive. Then I saw a very large, intimidating man get out of that tow truck. I saw tattoos, sunglasses covering his eyes, and biceps bigger than my head. He walked toward me at a rapid pace with his arm lifted. I suddenly felt really scared.

That upraised arm then landed gently on my shoulder. "Mr. Newton," he said, "I know this is hard and that you didn't plan for this. No one ever plans for their car to break down, do they?" I said, "Huh?" But he continued. "We will get through this together, Mr. Newton. I will make sure this mess gets all sorted out. I'll tow your truck to the dealership, and I will give you a ride home along the way."

His name was Walker, and this large, tattooed man was the embodiment of sensitivity and compassion. At one point, I looked at him and asked: "Walker, are you a Christian?" "No," he said, "I am a Libra."

Walker was very strange, indeed, and every bias, guess, and assumption I made about him turned out to be dead wrong.

I wonder: *could the same be true about God?* Is every bias, guess, and assumption we make about God wrong? When we "see" God through these biases, guesses, and assumptions, do we see anything worth seeing at all?

If we go with the flow of the world and, I hate to say this, the moralistic preaching and teaching that leaks out of far too many churches, the only thing we will see are spots: spots of fear, spots of greed, and spots of unredeemed pain. These spots always shrink us into a small person who protects with a terrified fierceness the little life we think is "ours." But according to the "real news," we don't have a life. Rather, Jesus Christ is Abundant and Eternal Life, and we are safely held in him—a different way of seeing altogether.

And so, if nothing else, I wrote this book to clean the lenses of our glasses and to remind us of what the real news is: namely,

Jesus Christ is the reckless love of God, God's Seed of Love sown into every crevice of creation, including that small bit we sometimes call "our life." I pray that this book will be an unexpected hand that lands gently on your shoulder, a compassionate voice saying, "We will get through this together." Perhaps it will be the saliva on your eyes, an experience of Jesus taking you by the hand and opening your eyes to a whole new world so that what Mark said of the blind man will be true for us, too: "His sight was restored, and he saw everything clearly" (Mark 8:25).

Chapter 1

Reckless

"Listen! A sower went out to sow. And as he sowed, some seed fell on the path, and the birds came and ate it up. Other seed fell on rocky ground, where it did not have much soil, and it sprang up quickly, since it had no depth of soil. And when the sun rose, it was scorched; and since it had no root, it withered away. Other seed fell among thorns, and the thorns grew up and choked it, and it yielded no grain. Other seed fell into good soil and brought forth grain, growing up and increasing and yielding thirty and sixty and a hundredfold." And he said, "Let anyone with ears to hear listen!" (Mark 4:3–9)

The first home I ever purchased had only one flaw: a barren front yard. I did not consider this to be a problem when I purchased the home, as I figured I would plant grass. However, I quickly learned that planting grass is hard. Recklessly throwing down a few squares of grass seed won't yield a plush green yard.

Planting grass, I later learned, would require loosening the ground and then meticulously raking the ground into a thousand little furrows. I would then need to scatter seed carefully and evenly. Next comes the wheat straw to hold in the moisture before watering, which of course is its own science. If you water the yard too much then the seeds will wash away, but if you fail to use enough water the seeds will never grow.

My front yard remained barren for the three years I lived in that house. I never planted the grass, but my research yielded loads of information about horticulture. I learned that a careful farmer is cautious and strategic, diligent and methodical, calculated and selective.

I find it shocking that Jesus's most famous parable is about a farmer who lacks these qualities. The farmer in Jesus's story is reckless. He throws seed around like it is confetti on New Year's Eve. Seed falls on the path, the thorns, the rocky ground, and some in good soil. The farmer in Jesus's story is wasteful and lavish and anything but calculated. The real shock comes when we discover who this farmer represents: God.

I used to believe that the purpose of this parable was to warn the faithful about the pitfalls of wealth and distraction. I read it as Jesus's way of encouraging me to be the good soil. Christians weren't supposed to be materialistic, shallow, and hard of heart like the rest of humanity, who represent the bad soil. This, I thought, was the parable's meaning—that a Christian has a calling to be good soil unlike the rest of the world; what Christianity offers is a road map on how to become good soil. This was a well-known truth in my church growing up.

Jesus did not tell parables to confirm well-known truths, but rather to shatter well-known truths.

When Jesus told the parable of the sower, everyone in his audience assumed they knew who God favored, that is, the "good" soil. God favored the right, the respectable, the religious, and people who kept the Law. This was well-known truth to anyone who knew anything about religion in Jesus's day. Only a fool would dare question this truth.

Was Jesus Christ himself such a fool?

On multiple times Jesus went on public record to state that God looked more like a reckless farmer than a stern and calculated judge. Jesus never spoke of a careful, cautious, strategic, diligent, methodical, calculated, and selective farmer looking only for the best soil to invest in. The God Jesus revealed looks more like the farmer in this parable: reckless with love, wasteful even, and in a terrific hurry to sow love wherever—simply because the nature of God is to sow love everywhere.

This is not a parable about good soil, but about a recklessly gracious Sower. It is a parable about a God that goes about recklessly sowing love wherever, irrespective of conditions. God, it seems, could not care less about return on investment.

Our experience of Christianity pivots on our understanding of this parable. "Do you not understand this parable?" Jesus asks. "Then how will you understand all the parables?" (Mark 4:13). If we get this parable wrong, we get the gospel wrong.

This is the question the parable of the sower confronts us with: do we know the reckless love of God that is perpetually poured out upon every human life and every ounce of creation in all seasons and conditions?

Imagine how exciting and transformative churches would be if they poured love into their community like the farmer in Jesus's parable. How spiritually rich and full of joy would our lives be if we loved and blessed the people in our lives with the same reckless abandon with which God blesses and loves us?

Becoming a reckless lover of all people is much like planting grass: easier said than done. We feel pain when our love falls on rocky, arid, or weed-infested ground. We want to give up and to stop loving when that happens. It hurts when the people we love don't love us back, and our great temptation is always to layer our heart in protective armor to ensure that we don't get hurt again. We hedge our bets by loving selectively and methodically. We are calculated lovers. We scout out the good soil and invest our love there.

The God we know in Jesus Christ refuses to love selectively. Jesus Christ, hanging naked from a cross with arms wide open, pronounced forgiveness on the mocking crowds. Jesus's whole life, indeed his every act, was a living display of the parable of the sower. Jesus Christ is God's Seed recklessly sown throughout the world. There is no corner of creation where this love is absent.

God's reckless love is counterintuitive. People who exhibit true inner goodness are precisely the people who have learned that they don't need an ounce of inner goodness for God to love them. These fortunate ones know that God recklessly and perpetually sows love into the lives of thorny, rocky, and hard-hearted people. They understand that only God's reckless love smooths the rocks, dulls the thorns, and softens the heart.

What might it take for you to begin living a less calculated, methodical life and to love a bit more indiscriminately and recklessly?

We extend reckless love to others only to the extent that we know and feel the reckless love that God has for each of us. We are empowered to sow seeds of love only to the extent that we know the One Seed, Jesus Christ, sowed throughout creation, buried deep beneath the earth, raised on that first Easter morning, and now bearing fruit throughout the world in preparation for a great harvest of love at the end of the age.

Discussion Questions

1. Why do you think Jesus spoke in parables? Do you think Jesus told parables to shatter well-known truths?
2. Do you believe that some people are "good soil" and that others are "bad soil"? Why or why not?
3. Do you believe that God is "reckless" with love? Can God be reckless and calculating at the same time?

Chapter 2

Forgiveness

He also told this parable to some who trusted in themselves that they were righteous and regarded others with contempt: "Two men went up to the temple to pray, one a Pharisee and the other a tax-collector. The Pharisee, standing by himself, was praying thus, 'God, I thank you that I am not like other people: thieves, rogues, adulterers, or even like this tax-collector. I fast twice a week; I give a tenth of all my income.' But the tax-collector, standing far off, would not even look up to heaven, but was beating his breast and saying, 'God, be merciful to me, a sinner!' I tell you, this man went down to his home justified rather than the other; for all who exalt themselves will be humbled, but all who humble themselves will be exalted." (Luke 18:9–14)

I have a confession: I love to sing, though I cannot carry a tune to save my life. In worship, I try to sit as close to the choir as possible so that no one can hear *me* sing. I want the nails-on-chalkboard croaking that some pastorally refer to as "my singing voice" to be drowned out by the loud, harmonious, and perfect voices of the gifted choir. With respect to musical ability, the choir is righteous and I am unrighteous. I may not be able to carry a tune, but when I sing next to the choir they always carry the tune for me.

I have not always been privy to the knowledge that my singing wasn't up to snuff. There was a time when I deemed myself a fabulous singer, and the long process of learning to tell the truth about my lack of musical ability has been rocky. One instance from seminary comes to mind. I was worshipping next to a friend, just singing my heart out, when he irritatingly nudged me during the service and asked me to sing a bit softer. I reminded him that the Bible teaches that God wants all people to make a joyful noise unto the Lord. "Not some people," I said smugly, "but all people." His reply was that, after hearing me sing, he was convinced that God could never will such a thing. I just assumed he was jealous of my vocal giftedness.

My self-image as a gifted singer finally crumbled last year. I was the guest preacher at a church—a routine Sunday visitation as far as diocesan work is concerned. During the offertory hymn, I sat in the chancel and sang my heart out. My eyes were closed, my voice was exalted, and I was making a loud and joyful noise to the Lord. I suddenly noticed that the rector was standing over me, frantically searching for something inside of my alb. I looked up to find that the congregation was lost in a fit of laughter. Most people had their faces buried in their hands trying to get the hysterics under control. My heart and my voice sank when I realized what the rector was trying to do: turn off my microphone. I had forgotten to turn off my lapel mike after my sermon, and suffice it to say that my amplified rendition of the descant in "Seek Ye First" was not preparing people's hearts for Holy Communion. In that moment, I was finally able to see myself accurately. I was not a gifted singer after all.

Jesus struggled mightily with religious types who refused to see themselves accurately. In Luke 18, one pious man stands out as being particularly blind. This Pharisee performs a host of respectable religious activities, but his heart isn't properly tuned in to the heart of God. Jesus tells this parable to remind us of something our hearts often refuse to admit: namely, that in the symphony of God's creation, *all* people are singing off-key. Furthermore, it is precisely the human race's tendency to sing off-key—whether we call this lack of attunement to God the human condition, sin, brokenness, fragmentation, or our shadow side—that Jesus came to heal in the most counterintuitive sort of way. Rather than offering encouragement, coaching, a law superior to that of Moses, or even motivation to try harder, Jesus "fixes" our dilemma by forgiving us. Jesus dies for the sins of the entire human race. Jesus offers us mercy, throws a party, and then invites us to do the same for one another.

The tax collector and all the other disreputable types in the Gospels loved Jesus's program of forgiveness. It was the religious establishment that gave Jesus pushback. Forgiveness struck them as unfair and regressive, threatening even, and I can't help but think that we often feel the same way. We love that God has forgiven us, but Hitler? Our ex-husband? Sex-trade traffickers?

We find forgiveness and mercy just as threatening as the religious types in Jesus's day. We love the *idea* of forgiveness, but when we have been wounded, or when we see the most vulnerable members of our population being wounded, the last thing we want to do is extend forgiveness. Forgiveness seems offensive and wrong. Our world teaches us to earn, achieve, perform, measure, count, evaluate, and weigh the evidence. It may be a harsh world, but we all know the rules of the game. We invest and expect a return. We earn and expect a reward. We give a little and we get a little. Good guys are rewarded, and bad guys are punished. Reciprocity keeps the old creation balanced. The mutual scratching of one another's back is all we know. Perhaps what makes Jesus so scandalous is his insistent and annoying reminder that all that we know is dead wrong with respect to the kingdom of God. Jesus refuses to play by the rules of our game.

Jesus's message of forgiveness and mercy for all will forever remain incomprehensible to a person who does not know that they are a sinner. When we admit that we are sinners, we do not make a moralistic judgment but a theological judgment. We number ourselves among those in need of mercy and forgiveness. We stand with the worst and call them brother and sister.

Talk of sin has become a stumbling block for many, most likely because of the word's baggage. We are accustomed to thinking of sin as bad conduct that can be overcome by knowledge, discipline, and prayer. The problem, of course, is that the Pharisee that Jesus lovingly critiques has built his whole life around knowledge, discipline, and prayer. His virtue is what blinds him to the reckless love of God.

The Bible never talks about sin as bad conduct that we can overcome. Sin is a condition from which we need to be rescued. In asking us to confess our sin, scripture and the Church are not trying to stir up feelings of shame and inadequacy. The irony of self-hatred is that it is a clever form of pride, a way of exalting ourselves. When we hate our self, or are ashamed of our self, we elevate how we feel about ourselves over what the Bible insists is true: namely, that we are recklessly loved by God and cherished in God's eyes, sheep for whom the Good Shepherd gladly laid down his life.

If we know that we are sinners, we know our need for rescue. We do not focus primarily on the world's need for rescue, or how deeply our coworker, spouse, or political leaders need to be rescued. Like the tax collector, we beat our breast and pray, "Lord, have mercy on me!" We come to see ourselves more accurately and we acknowledge the sin that infects our heart. In confession, I come to see that, ironically, my greatest problem is *me*.

In 1965, Flannery O'Connor published a short story called "Revelation." The main character in this story is Ruby Turpin, who, like the Pharisee in Luke's Gospel, is blinded by her virtue and doesn't see herself accurately. She can spot just about anyone's sin but her own. At the end of the story, Ruby has a revelation. She sees a vision of a road that runs from the earth to the sky where the souls of the redeemed are processing into heaven. This is how O'Connor describes Ruby's vision:

She saw . . . a vast swinging bridge extending upward from the earth through a field of living fire. Upon it a vast horde of souls were tumbling toward heaven . . . clean for the first time in their lives . . . battalions of freaks and lunatics shouting and clapping and leaping like frogs. And bringing up the end of the procession was a tribe of people whom [Ruby] recognized at once as those who, like herself . . . had always had a little of everything and the God-given wit to use it right. They were marching behind the others with great dignity. They alone were on key. Yet she could see by their shocked and altered faces that even their virtues were being burned away.[1]

In the Episcopal Church, our weekly worship culminates with the Holy Eucharist. We receive Christ's body and blood, and we profess by faith that in Christ we are forgiven, healed, and renewed. Ushers sometimes make sure that God's people come forward to the altar in good order. Episcopalians can be quiet and dignified in worship, and outwardly we are all "on key" as we come forward to receive the sacrament.

I always pray that people's souls are much *less* dignified than their outward appearance as they process forward to receive the Eucharist. I want people to acknowledge, just for once, that they are freaks and lunatics. God's people should clap, shout, and leap like frogs because they see themselves accurately and they know that they are loved, cherished, and saved by God. I want God to send a living fire to burn away anything that keeps us trusting in our self, even if that happens to be our virtue.

Where does your self-image need to crumble a bit? Where do you fear that long process of learning to tell the truth about yourself?

---

1. The short story "Revelation" is found in Flannery O'Connor, *Everything That Rises Must Converge* (New York: Farrar, Straus and Giroux, 1965), 191–244. I have shortened and modified the quote for the purposes of this text.

There is nothing to fear. We are all singing off-key, and it is only when we confess that truth—that we are sinners in need of rescue—that we awaken to see that God's reckless love is redeeming every broken note, every failure, every sin, and every heartbreak. God is weaving it all together into a glorious symphony that will echo for eternity in a new creation.

The reckless love of God in Jesus Christ is like a good choir. Morally speaking, we just can't carry a tune, but Jesus can carry it for us. The prophet Zephaniah says God "rejoices over us with very loud singing."[2] All people, whether they know it or not, are washed in that song. Every one of us has been forgiven. Forgiveness is not a moral or spiritual matter. Forgiveness is a *political* matter. It is the one law that fuels the new creation, the kingdom of God.

Discussion Questions

1. Do you believe that God has forgiven all people of their sins? Is there anyone you wish that God would not forgive?
2. Do you find it difficult to forgive others? To forgive yourself? If so, what makes forgiveness so difficult?
3. Can our "virtue" ever present an obstacle to knowing and serving God? Why or why not?

---

2. Zeph. 3:17.

Chapter 3

Beggars

The apostles said to the Lord, "Increase our faith!" The Lord replied, "If you had faith the size of a mustard seed, you could say to this mulberry tree, 'Be uprooted and planted in the sea,' and it would obey you. Who among you would say to your slave who has just come in from plough-ing or tending sheep in the field, 'Come here at once and take your place at the table'? Would you not rather say to him, 'Prepare supper for me, put on your apron and serve me while I eat and drink; later you may eat and drink'? Do you thank the slave for doing what was commanded? So you also, when you have done all that you were ordered to do, say, 'We are worthless slaves; we have done only what we ought to have done!'" (Luke 17:5–10)

Assisi is a stunningly beautiful little town in Italy. It also was the home of the twelfth-century monk and saint we know as Francis. I went on a pilgrimage to Assisi a few years ago, where I studied Francis's life. In my visit to the holy sites associated with his call, I learned that God spoke three words into the depth of Francis's soul that changed his life forever: *repair my church.*

Upon hearing these words, Francis renounced his wealth and was disowned by his father. Francis built bridges of peace with the Muslim world, preached the gospel to humans and animals alike, founded a monastery, and lived in solidarity with the poor. His impact on the church was so significant that Francis was canonized a saint only two years after his death. I was awestruck by Francis's faith. My time in Assisi left me with a burning desire for more faith, and I just assumed that *more* faith was needed if God could use me to repair God's church.

My heart aches for God's church to be repaired. I long for God's reckless love to fill the earth and for the church to become a conduit through which God's healing, justice, and grace flow out into the world. I want the universal body of God's wonderfully diverse people—who confess with their mouths that Jesus is Lord and who believe in their heart that God raised Jesus from the dead—to grow their capacity to love other people more recklessly. Bruised and scared people do not flock to the church the way they flocked to Jesus, and Christians don't seek out hurting human beings the way Francis and Jesus did. God's call to Francis echoes in the hearts and minds of many Christians today: *repair my church.*

When I feel God's desire to repair the church and to use me as a vessel in that holy and miraculous work, my gut reaction is always to pray alongside the apostles that God would increase my faith. The problems we face are complex, and I often feel inadequate and confused about what needs to be done or even how I should go about doing what I know needs to get done. With respect to faith, I feel like I have five loaves and two fish. There is barely enough food for me to eat, let alone enough to feed the world's multitudes. I want to do God's work, but I feel like I need more faith, more time, more energy, more passion, more eloquence, more courage, and more everything. "God," I pray, "increase my faith!"

I love that Jesus responds to the apostles' request by not taking it too seriously. Instead, Jesus gives them a ridiculous scenario to imagine where, if they only had more faith, they could run around uprooting trees with their words and casting those same trees into the sea.

Jesus rejects the foundational assumption on which the apostles' prayer is based, namely that more faith is better and that the disciples do not have enough. We think that Jesus is disappointed that their faith is so weak, small, and fragile. This is a natural and automatic way of thinking, simply because we are conditioned to expect a steady dose of judgment from the Bible. This interpretation of Jesus's words, however, could not be more wrong.

Jesus's response to their prayer is not shaming and angry, and given that the apostles have already quit their jobs and left their families to follow Jesus, I can only imagine that Jesus is deeply proud of how much faith they have already shown. Jesus does not speak sharp words of exhortation. These are playful words of banter from a man who will soon die for his friends. Jesus wants the apostles to lighten up. He understands that when we pile on too much of anything, even a good thing, it leaves us feeling heavier. From Jesus's perspective, heaviness is a problem because his yoke is easy and his burden is light (see Matt. 11:30).

Jesus responds to an absurd request with an absurd image. "You want *more* faith?" Jesus asks (wink, wink). "That's a great idea," Jesus says sarcastically, "because if I inject your faith with some holy steroids from on high you could run around uprooting trees with your words (because as we all know, the world has too many trees). With all this mega faith you would be invulnerable, powerful, and confident. You could repair the world, not by going to the cross (who has time for that), but by manipulating things with your words—that is, safely and from a distance."

Jesus was a master teacher, often using humor and irony, parable and prose, anger and compassion to instill in his followers a vision of God's paradoxical kingdom. Jesus wants to open our eyes to something that most of us miss most of the time: in the kingdom of God, the way up is the way down, life is about death, and growth happens not through increase but through decrease.

I struggle with Jesus's way of the cross and with the many ways that Jesus's values subvert my own. Frankly, I like the idea of possessing spiritual power. Uprooting trees with my words sounds fun. I assume that such a talent would make me important and respected. Part of me wants Jesus to turn stones to bread and let me do the same. My prayer for more faith is always a self-centered disguise, a way of asking God to take away my uncertainty, fear, and ambiguity. In other words, it's not so much that I want more faith. I just want God to take away the ambiguity and tension that life always brings. "Increase my faith" really means "decrease my cross." I don't want faith, really. I want control and confidence and to feel spiritually invulnerable. I want to uproot trees with my words, not to serve.

Francis once said, "I have been in all things unholy. If God can use me, God can use absolutely anyone."[3] It is easy to assume that Francis had tons of faith, much more than you and me. Francis never saw himself this way, and there were many moments when he felt weak, uncertain, inadequate, and scared. His life teaches me that people who feel spiritually invulnerable and confident cannot repair God's church. Grace flows to the world only through people who are weak and often uncertain and who cling to Jesus in their experience of decreasing and becoming *less.*

What saves the world and repairs the church is never our faith, but the faithfulness of Jesus Christ. Faith can't be a quantity that we possess as individuals, a substance that we accumulate and measure how much we have relative to someone else. There is no invisible faith meter buried in our chest that we learn to crank up from icy cold to burning hot over a lifetime.[4] Once we rid ourselves of the superstition that God is watching

---

3. http://celticfranciscanmonk.com/?cat=14.
4. I borrow the image of the "faith meter" from the late Robert Capon.

and monitoring some invisible faith meter, the silly idea that we need more faith can fall into the sea, presumably somewhere next to the mulberry tree.

What then do we say to that inner, anxious apostle that prays and pleads with the Lord for more faith? What word of grace do we speak to that part of us that feels inadequate and that we need to be more than we currently are? I listen to Francis. "God," he once prayed, "grant me the treasure of sublime poverty: permit the distinctive sign of our order to be that it does not possess anything of its own and that it has no other patrimony than begging."[5]

It is not wrong to pray for more faith. However, if we find that the answer to our prayer makes us less of a beggar and not more of one, I suggest that we pray for something else. God does not repair the church by making us more, but by making us less; not with big, showy gestures of faith, but with small and consistent acts of love. It is never the greatness of our faith that repairs the church and the world, but the greatness of Christ's faithfulness to fulfill God's promise.

It is more than enough to show up to the life we have been given to steward with our uncertainty, vulnerability, and fear and to do small things with great love, care, and service. Francis did not have a faith that uprooted trees, but a faith that sang with animals, clothed the poor, and loved people that no one else would love. It was a small faith that Francis received moment by moment, because he knew that he was a beggar and that faith was a gift from God.

Discussion Questions

1. Do you ever feel like you do not have enough faith? Is it possible to have too much faith? Why or why not?

---

5. http://www.historyofpainters.com/francis.htm.

2. In what sense do you believe that God's church needs to be "repaired" in today's world? Where do you see this good work happening?

3. "The essence of faith is begging." Do you agree? Why or why not?

Chapter 4

Baptism

Then Jesus came from Galilee to John at the Jordan, to be baptized by him. John would have prevented him, saying, "I need to be baptized by you, and do you come to me?" But Jesus answered him, "Let it be so now; for it is proper for us in this way to fulfill all righteousness." Then he consented. And when Jesus had been baptized, just as he came up from the water, suddenly the heavens were opened to him and he saw the Spirit of God descending like a dove and alighting on him. And a voice from heaven said, "This is my Son, the Beloved, with whom I am well pleased." (Matt. 3:13–17)

Reckless love is not an idea, a doctrine, or an attempt to rebrand Christianity. It is not an emerging, progressive, postmodern, post-evangelical, Jesus-centric spirituality. Reckless love is not a gimmick, but a reality that lies at the heart of our universe. God *is* reckless love: the Father, Son, and Spirit in a circular dance of mutual self-emptying and receiving, an emptiness and fullness that draws us into a life of participation. Jesus was baptized to draw us into that reckless love. Through Jesus, we are incorporated and drawn into the mystery of this one life.

Baptism is a sacrament for people who identify with sinners. John the Baptist proclaimed a "baptism of repentance for the forgiveness of sins" (Mark 1:4). According to both scripture and tradition, Jesus was *not* a sinner. Jesus was like us in all respects, "yet without sin" (Heb. 4:15).

Jesus's baptism marked the very beginning of his public ministry. Before his baptism, Jesus lived a quiet life, presumably working as a carpenter in Nazareth. With Jesus's baptism, he goes public as Israel's expected Messiah. It is Jesus's manifesto, a public and symbolic statement about the nature of his mission and ministry.

In more recent times another man came forth out of anonymity into action: Father Damien. Born Joseph de Veuster, he lived in the late nineteenth century in Belgium and answered a call to the religious profession with a mission to serve in Hawaii. In the 1860s the Hawaiian legislature passed a bill called the "Act to Prevent the Spread of Leprosy." The impact of this bill was that some eight thousand people were banished to a leper colony. When Father Damien heard this news, it caused him great grief and he was moved with compassion. Damien left the comfort of where he was and chose to make his home among the lepers.[6]

For twenty years, Damien embraced, loved, and served this group of sick, banished, and forgotten people. Damien offered them dignity, connection, physical touch, and a sense of their inherent worth. So closely did he identify with these lepers that on a Sunday morning in 1885 Father Damien opened his sermon with two astonishing words: *we lepers*.

Damien was desperate for these lepers to know that he did not think of himself as being above them. Damien's mission was to stand with them in their disease so that he might offer them healing and hope.

When Jesus was baptized by John in the Jordan River, alongside people that society did not respect or love or value, I believe

---

6. www.franciscanmedia.org/saint-damien-de-veuster-of-moloka-i/ (accessed September 6, 2017).

that Jesus Christ was making a very similar statement: *we sinners.* As Israel's long-awaited Messiah, Jesus would fully identify with all of humanity, and not just the people of Israel. In Jesus, God's reckless love would be lavished onto all and not some, not from above but from the very bottom by a Messiah who chose to stand *with* humanity.

If our baptism fully identifies us with God, Jesus's baptism unveils God's desire to fully identify with us. Jesus willingly joined himself to sinful humanity so that sinful humanity might be fully joined, fully united, to God.

Jesus is not a mere good example, as if a role model were all that humanity needed. There would be nothing reckless about God sending humanity a role model. Such a move on God's part would be utterly predictable, boring, common, ineffective, and utterly lacking in surprise. Christianity does not teach that God so loved the world that he sent a role model, but that God so loved the world that he sent his Son.

Damien became a leper and the Son became a sinner, both examples of a love so reckless that our minds can barely fathom it. In his baptism, Jesus preached a two-word sermon: *we sinners.* "I have not come to stand above you," Jesus said, "but I have come to stand with you in your disease."

Irenaeus, a second-century theologian, put it like this: "Out of his boundless love, Christ became what we are, so that we might become what He is."[7] The apostle Paul writes something similar in 2 Corinthians: "God made him who knew no sin to be sin for us, so that in him we might become the righteousness of God."[8] Jesus became what we are so that we might become what he is—an embodiment of reckless love.

The words our Creator spoke over Jesus are the same words that every human being is desperate to hear: "This is my son (or daughter), my beloved, with whom I am well pleased." People

---

7. Irenaeus, *Against Heresies*, V.
8. 2 Cor. 5:21.

build their entire lives around trying to earn these words from someone they respect or admire, usually their parents or parental figures. We are always unconsciously (or consciously) seeking to earn a blessing. *How can I be accepted? How can I be loved? What must I do for people to be well pleased with me?*

Our performance-driven world's answer to these questions is disheartening. Do something that is pleasing first; receive the very conditional and fragile blessing second. Be funny. Be smart. Get a tattoo. Make money. Be outgoing. Don't have a bad game. Stand out, be unique, make a difference, get your ducks in a row, don't be boring, do something pleasing, and only *after* you perform will people love you and accept you. Maybe. That's just the way things work in this world. We do something pleasing first. We experience love and belonging second. It's called conditional love, and it eats us alive.

Jesus's baptism represents a complete reversal of that order. Baptism means that there is no condition to God's reckless and limitless and uncalculated love. We don't behave to belong. We simply believe that we eternally and unconditionally belong to God. God is deeply pleased with us no matter what. We cling to God's grace-full promise in faith and as we believe, we increasingly embody the sort of life that God intends us to live. Reckless love starts spilling out—from God first and from us second.

Jesus's baptism was revolutionary because it replaced conventional religion with the gospel. Conventional religion says, "Do something well pleasing, and then maybe God will accept you." The gospel, however, doesn't comprehend the word *maybe*. It is all "yes" in Christ (see 2 Cor. 1:20). In Christ, we are already and eternally acceptable. The point of faith is merely to grasp our belovedness and to be dazzled.

The prophet Isaiah writes: "Surely he has borne our infirmities and carried our diseases."[9] I am reminded not just of Jesus, but also of Father Damien. By the time he died, Father Damien

---

9. Isaiah 53:4.

had contracted leprosy. In living he felt called to give these sick, banished, and forgotten people something that had been taken from them: dignity, worth, love, belonging, and a sense that someone was "well pleased" enough with them to embrace them, to love them, and to get close. Metaphorically speaking, Father Damien stood *with them* in the Jordan. Out of his boundless love, he had to become what they were—a leper—so that they might become fully human.

Why was Jesus baptized?

It depends on how we view our selves. If all we really need is a good example or a little ego boost—assuming that's what Jesus provides—then Jesus's baptism remains a puzzle. However, if Jesus was right in saying, "Those who are well have no need of a physician but only those who are sick,"[10] and if despite the myriad ways we try to convince the world that we're all just fine where what we really need is a savior, then Jesus's baptism is nothing less than God making a statement to the world that he came to embrace us, love us, get close, and bear our disease for us, even to the point of dying on a cross.

Discussion Questions

1. Why do you think Jesus was baptized? What do you see as the theological significance of your own baptism?
2. What is the main difference between God's approval and the approval offered by our world? Is one more "conditional" than the other? Why or why not?
3. What similarities do you see between Damien's life and Jesus's life? What differences?

---

10. Mark 2:17.

Chapter 5

Saints

When Jesus saw the crowds, he went up the mountain; and after he sat down, his disciples came to him. Then he began to speak, and taught them, saying: "Blessed are the poor in spirit, for theirs is the kingdom of heaven. Blessed are those who mourn, for they will be comforted. Blessed are the meek, for they will inherit the earth. Blessed are those who hunger and thirst for righteousness, for they will be filled. Blessed are the merciful, for they will receive mercy. Blessed are the pure in heart, for they will see God. Blessed are the peacemakers, for they will be called children of God. Blessed are those who are persecuted for righteousness' sake, for theirs is the kingdom of heaven." (Matt. 5:1–10)

A friend recently expressed his admiration that I was called to the priesthood. He made it clear that he was relieved that God hadn't called *him* to such a vocation, but he was glad that I heeded God's call. My friend calls himself an "ordinary believer," and he doesn't believe that people "like him" are called to meaningful ministry. "I'm no saint," he repeated, as if it were his mantra.

The first time I ever heard the word *saint* was during a chapel service when I was in the first grade. The minister talked about several ancient figures that the church now considers to be saints. He talked about Saint Peter, who was crucified upside down. We learned about Stephen who was stoned to death. In story after story, I heard about these people called "saints" who left their family, renounced their wealth, experienced martyrdom, and lived alone in a cell where they prayed all day but never got to eat a meal. This was a lot to take in for a first grader. I had seen horror movies that scared me less than this chapel service. When the service concluded, the minister exhorted us to be diligent in our prayers so that maybe God would make us a saint, too. That settled it. I didn't say a prayer for another three years.

My understanding of what it meant to be a saint changed over time, though not necessarily for the better. In high school, I believed that a saint was a good, disciplined, and holy person. Much like my friend, I believed that saints were a special class of humans who knew God's rules and followed them. I envisioned God as being like a talent scout on a quest to find the best moral athletes, or saints, who were holy enough to further the divine cause. In my mind, it was a two-dimensional world and church. There were ordinary believers like my friend, and then there were saints. I assumed that ordinary believers were not called to do whatever it is that saints were called to do. I did not think that ordinary believers were condemned; I just imagined that saints were especially blessed. Ordinary believers lived life in the valley, but the saint's dwelling was on the mountaintop.

Mountains are noted frequently in the Bible; they dotted the geography where the People of God lived and travelled. God was believed to dwell "above" in the heavens (sky), on mountaintops, and in the clouds. One often had to climb a mountain to be close to God. God gave Israel, through Moses, the Law on Mount Sinai. Mountaintops, biblically speaking, are powerful symbols of God's presence and God's Law. When Israel lived in the wilderness, only the virtuous were invited to climb God's mountain. No one accompanied Moses when he received the Ten Commandments because ordinary believers were not allowed to climb. Consider the words of the psalmist: "Who may ascend the mountain of the Lord?" He asks this only to answer his own question: "The one who has clean hands and a pure heart . . . will receive a blessing from the Lord."[11] It's easy to read into the Bible a two-dimensional world where ordinary believers live life in the valley but saints, a special subset of the faithful, can climb the mountain to receive a blessing from God.

Each of us, in our own way, understands what a spiritual life stuck in the valley feels like. We look in the mirror and we see an ordinary believer, a person we assume God can't use to make a positive, love-spreading difference in the world. We don't always feel like our hands are clean and our hearts are pure. We're not certain that we've been invited to climb the mountain and receive a blessing from the Lord. Few of us feel like we are especially blessed and live our life with an eager readiness to extend God's blessing to others.

Jesus began his ministry by climbing a mountain. Consider Israel's history: only Moses, Elijah, and on rare occasions a few others could climb a mountain to speak with God. It is stunning that Jesus invites all people to trek up a mountain with him to receive God's blessing. "Blessed are the poor in spirit," he says. "Blessed are those who mourn. Blessed are the meek. Blessed are those who hunger and thirst for righteousness."

"Blessed. Blessed. Blessed. Blessed," Jesus says. "For theirs is the kingdom of heaven."

Jesus's blessings are so revolutionary and countercultural that most of us fail to understand them. They make zero sense to our performance-driven world. Jesus announces that the kingdom of heaven has been thrown open to all and that everyone is

---

11. Psalm 24:3–5, NIV.

especially blessed. Jesus destroys the idea of a two-dimensional world; "saints" and "ordinary believers" are equal in God's eyes.

If we read Jesus's Beatitudes carefully, nothing we do earns or merits the blessing that Jesus speaks over us.[12] For instance, being "poor in spirit" is not a virtue. The poor in spirit are spiritually bankrupt, and God does not bless people because they are poor in spirit. Nor does God bless anyone because they mourn. Those who mourn are brokenhearted. They have been paralyzed by rejection and gut-wrenched by grief. Meekness is also not a virtue. The meek are shy and intimidated, and they often don't know how to stand up for themselves. Meekness is not a precondition for God's blessing.

I concede that it is good to be merciful, pure in heart, and to live as a peacemaker. However, we are not blessed *because* these qualities may describe us. There is nothing we can do to earn God's special blessing. We are blessed because the kingdom of heaven has been thrown open to all, and in God's kingdom *all* people are especially blessed.

There isn't such a thing as a two-dimensional church. God's reckless love is sown into the lives of all people. As our baptismal liturgy begins in the Episcopal Church, "There is one Body and one Spirit. There is one hope in God's call to us."[13] In the kingdom of God, there are not two dimensions or bodies, but one.

We are all on the mountaintop with Jesus right now. God's reckless love has brought us there together. A saint *knows* she lives on that mountaintop as a gift of grace and she has chosen to root her life in God's unconditional blessing.

When you wake up tomorrow and look in the mirror, I hope you don't see an ordinary believer, because there's no such thing. Instead, I pray you see God's image-bearer who is especially

---

12. The term *beatitude* derives from the Latin *beātitūdō* meaning "happiness." Matthew 5:3–12 are often called "the Beatitudes."
13. Book of Common Prayer, 299. This portion of the liturgy is quoting Paul's letter to the Ephesians.

blessed in your mourning and poverty of spirit and in your hunger and thirst for completion. Make God's special blessing the foundation of your life and be creative and courageous in your willingness to extend that blessing to others. There are far too many people in our world who have never been told that the mountaintop is also for them.

Discussion Questions

1. What does the word saint mean to you? Is a saint something you are, or something you become?
2. How does one root his or her life in God's unconditional blessing? What spiritual practices do you rely on to help you know God's blessing in your own life?
3. People sometimes speak of their "mountaintop experience." Have you ever had such an experience? Is the mountaintop a place we visit from time to time or a place where we can learn to live?

Chapter 6

Faith

Now when Jesus came into the district of Caesarea Philippi, he asked his disciples, "Who do people say that the Son of Man is?" And they said, "Some say John the Baptist, but others Elijah, and still others Jeremiah or one of the prophets." He said to them, "But who do you say that I am?" Simon Peter answered, "You are the Messiah, the Son of the living God." And Jesus answered him, "Blessed are you, Simon son of Jonah! For flesh and blood has not revealed this to you, but my Father in heaven. And I tell you, you are Peter, and on this rock I will build my church, and the gates of Hades will not prevail against it. I will give you the keys of the kingdom of heaven, and whatever you bind on earth will be bound in heaven, and whatever you loose on earth will be loosed in heaven." (Matt. 16:13–19)

"What do you want us to *do* because of this sermon?" A kind church lady recently asked me this question after a Sunday service where I was the guest preacher. She seemed baffled by my answer: "How am I supposed to know?"

I'm not big on exhorting, persuading, or calling people to action when I preach, and I rarely offer an application or a "takeaway." I simply remind people that they are in Christ, and that Christ is in them, and I trust the Spirit with the outcomes.

I don't believe that the Christian life is passive, but only that God has already completed all the essential work that needs completing. The moment we comprehend God's finished work, we find ourselves being worked on by God, an epiphany that transforms the way we engage other people and even ourselves. "This is the work of God," Jesus said, "that you believe in him whom God has sent" (John 6:29). Our work is to believe, or to have faith.

People assume that our faith creates a relationship with God, or that God lavishes God's goodness onto us after we profess faith in Jesus. Not only does this frame faith in transactional terms, it gives the appearance that God's love is a reward for our faith. However, our faith is always the fruit of God's reckless love. Our faith does not precede God's lavish love. On the contrary, God's loving gaze creates our faith. When we profess faith in Jesus a new relationship is not created that hitherto did not exist. Rather, a relationship that has existed from the foundation of the world is acknowledged and made conscious. God opens our eyes and we awaken to deeper levels of intimacy with God (see Ephesians 1:4).

Think of it this way. Let's say that a week before you move into a new home I sneak in and bury a million dollars in cash under a floorboard in your living room. I then give you a call and present you with the good news that a million dollars comes with your new home, no strings attached. You may believe this news, or you may reject the news as being a fantasy. Or you may not have a cell phone and never receive the message in the first place. But you're a millionaire either way. I don't give you the money after you believe the news. Rather, when you say, "I believe," you begin to enjoy the riches that are already yours to begin with.

Faith in Jesus Christ doesn't create a relationship. Faith doesn't earn you brownie points with God or change your status on the heavenly rolls. Faith is always a response to a reckless love we call the Trinity that has always been present in your life. Faith is a waking up, an "aha," a newfound capacity that enables us to enjoy the gift of being alive in God's enchanted world.

One of the things that most upset the religious establishment in Jesus's day was that the people who professed faith in Him were mostly disreputable folk—fishermen, hookers, tax collectors, lepers, and the like. Jesus told these untouchables that the keys to God's kingdom already belonged to them and, for the most part, they believed him.

One might think that the Messiah would be more discriminate and discerning with respect to choosing his leadership team. Jesus didn't seem concerned with return on investment. After all, Jesus gives the keys to the kingdom of heaven to Peter. Peter, you may recall, is the disciple who always missed the point, who put his foot in his mouth on several occasions, who cut off someone's ear in the Garden of Gethsemane, and who denied even knowing Jesus in his most profound time of need. Peter received a pair of keys he didn't earn, deserve, or even understand.

The call of God is not connected to our merits whatsoever. As I "grow" in faith, I find that I am as sinful, stubborn, and selfish as I was when I first dropped my net to follow Jesus. Our mission is not to clean ourselves up, but to bear witness to God's reckless love in our mess. Christians do not stand in this world from a place of moral superiority. The people Jesus had the most beef with were precisely the religious types who felt superior to others who lacked their same devotion.

Augustine was once asked by a seeker what he could expect if he went to church. He apparently responded by saying, "Drunkards, misers, tricksters, gamblers, adulterers, fornicators, and assiduous clients of sorcerers."[14] Augustine's point is that Jesus does not hand us the keys to the kingdom of heaven

---

14. www.christianitytoday.com/history/2008/august/st-mugg-and-wrestling-prophets.html.

because we are good. Our authority and mission have zero, zilch, nada, to do with our merits, goodness, or spiritual resume. Rather, our authority is rooted in our continual willingness to confess that Jesus Christ is Lord. The implication of this confession is that we are *not* the lords of the cosmos.

The late Henry Nouwen once said, "The world around us is saying in a loud voice, we can take care of ourselves. We do not need God or the Church. We are in control. And if we are not, we have to work harder to get in control. But beneath all the great accomplishments there is a deep current of despair. Broken relationships, boredom, and depression fill the hearts of millions."[15] Nouwen's point is that human beings are not wired to bear the burden of Godhood. The first thing God asks us to relinquish when we confess Jesus as Lord is the burden that comes with trying to control and manipulate the world. Such a confession is the very key that can unlock a whole new world of freedom, grace, and love.

"Who do you say that I am?" This is a question that Jesus asks each one of us. It is a question that asks us to profess what we believe to be true about God, about Jesus, about the kingdom of God, and about the hope of the world. When we confess Jesus Christ as Lord, a new and holy space is created in our heart that enables us to become a conduit through which God's reckless love flows into us and back out into the world. When we say, "You are the Christ!" the keys are handed to us, or perhaps more accurately we awaken to the mystery that we have been in possession of the keys from the foundation of the world.

A friend recently told me that the words *decide* and *homicide* derive from the same root. When we decide for something we simultaneously decide against, or we kill, something else. Every

---

15. This is a condensed and shortened quote from Nouwen's *In the Name of Jesus: Reflections on Christian Leadership* (Chestnut Ridge, NY: Crossroad Publishing Company, 1989), 19–21. The quote is not exact, but it captures the full essence of what Nouwen was trying to say.

"yes" to one thing is always a "no" to some other thing. Faith in Jesus is about saying "yes" to God's call to love the world as recklessly as He did and about saying "no" to being the calculated grudge-holders that we all too easily become when the world's rules shape our thinking, feeling, and acting.

The keys to the kingdom have been handed to Peter, to you, to me, to your crazy Aunt Sally, to the homeless guy you pass on your way to work, to your political rivals, and to anyone else you can imagine. The one thing each human being shares is that God loves each one of us madly and that for reasons unbeknownst to us God has decided to hand us the keys to the kingdom simply because God thinks it a swell idea. The million dollars is already under our floorboard and the One who put it there asks: Who do *you* say that I am?

Discussion Questions

1. What does the word faith mean to you? Do you believe that faith creates a relationship with God? Why or why not?
2. Does faith in God come naturally to you? When in your life have you found faith to be most difficult?
3. Can one be intentional about growing in one's faith? If so, how?

Chapter 7

Discipleship

At that time Jesus said, "I thank you, Father, Lord of heaven and earth, because you have hidden these things from the wise and the intelligent and have revealed them to infants; yes, Father, for such was your gracious will. All things have been handed over to me by my Father; and no one knows the Son except the Father, and no one knows the Father except the Son and anyone to whom the Son chooses to reveal him. Come to me, all you that are weary and are carrying heavy burdens, and I will give you rest. Take my yoke upon you, and learn from me; for I am gentle and humble in heart, and you will find rest for your souls. For my yoke is easy, and my burden is light." (Matt. 11:25–30)

The week after my ordination was among the most awkward times of my life. I was a twenty-six-year-old deacon and soon-to-be priest, and the parishioners I was commissioned to serve routinely confused me with one of the high school sophomores from the church youth group. I also felt awkward wearing a clergy collar, which looks like a white plastic ring that circles the neck. It is about an inch wide and typically worn with a black clergy shirt.

Aside from my feeling socially awkward, the clergy collar was uncomfortable, and it felt very restrictive. Wearing this collar reminded me of an experience I had doing mission work in Burma while in seminary. In a car that broke down on the side of the road, we passed the time watching oxen work the fields. Each ox had a yoke around its neck, a wooden crossbeam held in place by a combination of poles, hooks, and chains. For thousands of years, people have used yokes to force recalcitrant animals to work the land.

In biblical times, the yoke was a symbol vested with a lot of religious significance. Every rabbi in Jesus's day had his own "yoke." A rabbi's yoke was his rules, or his list, of what a disciple was required to do to maintain his relationship with God. Put differently, a rabbi's yoke was the teaching he imparted to his students on what it meant to be faithful to the God of Israel.

A respectable rabbi wouldn't just take anyone as his student. If a man wanted to be under the tutelage of a rabbi, he had to be determined, intelligent, and in the right social class. He couldn't be deformed or unclean, and women and children were ruled out automatically. However, if a rabbi accepted you as his student, you could proudly tell others that you had made the cut and taken up Rabbi So-and-so's yoke.

Many of the rabbis in Jesus's day were Pharisees, a religious group that Jesus criticized because they placed heavy and unbearable burdens on the shoulders of others (see Matt. 23:4). The yoke of the Pharisees was heavy, and they taught their students a straightforward list of tedious rules and regulations. In their mind, the keeping of God's rules was more important to God than the very human beings those rules were meant to serve. The Pharisees had a long list. This list was their yoke, their religion, and their salvation. God, it seems, was nothing more than a miserly bookkeeper—a deity whose favor was won or lost depending on how well one kept God's list.

The specific sect within Judaism known as the Pharisees may be extinct, but the religion of the list is stronger than ever. How we feel about our relationship with God so often ebbs and flows with how well we think we have kept God's list. Maybe we have a list of things we think we should be doing, such as attending church, reading the Bible, or tithing more of our money. Or maybe we feel guilty because we keep doing things we assume are on God's list of what we should not be doing. Either way, we have a knee-jerk tendency to measure our standing with God based on how well we have kept our list. We also typically have some list we use to evaluate and judge other people. This religion of the list is rigged against us. Our list is too big and our ability is too small. The yoke of the Pharisees, the religion of the list, always leaves us feeling ashamed, alone, scared, and depressed.

There is a question that we must consciously, repetitively, and fearlessly answer if we hunger to experience and share the reckless love of God that we know in Jesus Christ: whose yoke have *we* taken on? In other words, who is our teacher? Who do we trust to give us the best information about life, love, and meaning, and about how to live our lives in God's great world?

Our world is full of people eager to hand us a list—our parents and friends, our politicians and priests, Oprah and *Us Weekly*. Some of these lists are subtle, and some are not so subtle, but every teacher has his or her list. A list tells us what to believe and what to value, how to feel, what to eat, and the best way to spend our time. Some of the lists are good, and some will probably kill us. But this is beside the point: *Jesus Christ doesn't have a list*. Christian discipleship is not about rules but about a relationship; not about principles but about a Person; not about a list but about love.

The Pharisees were so boring—they all had the exact same list, and their pattern was utterly predictable. The Pharisees would weed out the unclean, chase away the riffraff, and then hand people a list that was impossible to keep. I can scarcely imagine how shocked, baffled, relieved, and threatened people were by the emergence of a rabbi named Jesus who did not have a list. He walked the streets with a motley crew of prostitutes and lepers, women and men, children and adults, fishermen and tax collectors. Rabbi Jesus embodied the inclusivity that is the reckless love of God. "Come to me *all*," Jesus said, while other rabbis only accepted a limited number of applications. This peculiar rabbi's yoke wasn't hard. "My yoke is easy," he said, and "my burden is light."

Our world is all too eager to place a heavy, ill-fitting yoke onto us, and not everyone knows that there is such a thing as an easy yoke. In a performance-driven world, Jesus's yoke will always seem foolish and naïve to intelligent folk who seek salvation in their list. Jesus said that his yoke would only make sense if we learned to become an infant. An infant is completely dependent upon others for protection and support, for love and for meaning. What makes infants wonderful is that they know their utter dependence. I've never seen an infant try to get a job or cook a meal. When loved and cared for by their parents, infants are open and trusting, dependent and playful, simple and expectant. As Frederick Buechner states:

> We are children, perhaps, at the very moment when we know that it is as children that God loves us—not because we have deserved his love and not in spite of our undeserving; not because we try and not because we recognize the futility of our trying; but simply because he has chosen to love us. We are children because he is our father; and all of our efforts, fruitful and fruitless, to do good, to speak truth, to understand, are the efforts of children who, for all their precocity, are children still in that before we loved him, he loved us, as children, through Jesus Christ our lord.[16]

The yoke of Jesus makes sense only when we acknowledge that we are children whom God adores. It feels vulnerable to acknowledge our utter dependence on God and each other.

---

16. Frederick Buechner, *The Magnificent Defeat* (New York: HarperCollins, 1966), 135.

Lists are so seductive and common because they feel safe and reinforce our illusions of control. Jesus, on the other hand, is anything but safe. It is risky and vulnerable to live in union with Jesus Christ. The yoke of Jesus may be easy, but it always leads to wild and unexpected places.

I think back on those oxen I watched for hours in Burma, miserable as they bore the heavy burden of someone else's work. Jesus does not want us to feel like those oxen. We are not forced to work for Jesus, for we have been afforded the privilege to work *with* Jesus. Yokes don't have to be hard, heavy, or a burden, because one rabbi dared to claim that his yoke was easy.

Discussion Questions

1. Is there a heavenly list of what God expects from God's disciples? Do you have a list of what you expect from yourself with respect to God? If so, does your list offer you comfort? Why or why not?
2. What do you think it means to receive the kingdom of God as "a child"? In what sense are we called to be childlike with respect to our faith? To *not* be childlike with respect to our faith?
3. What do you think most distinguished Jesus from other rabbis in his day? What about Jesus do you think most angered the religious establishment?

Chapter 8

Repentance

Then the Pharisees went and plotted to entrap him in what he said. So they sent their disciples to him, along with the Herodians, saying, "Teacher, we know that you are sincere, and teach the way of God in accordance with truth, and show deference to no one; for you do not regard people with partiality. Tell us, then, what you think. Is it lawful to pay taxes to the emperor, or not?" But Jesus, aware of their malice, said, "Why are you putting me to the test, you hypocrites? Show me the coin used for the tax." And they brought him a denarius. Then he said to them, "Whose head is this, and whose title?" They answered, "The emperor's." Then he said to them, "Give therefore to the emperor the things that are the emperor's, and to God the things that are God's." When they heard this, they were amazed; and they left him and went away. (Matt. 22:15–22)

On the tail end of spring break during my sophomore year of college I recall driving to Austin, Texas. As I neared the city, I encountered a lethal combo of rush hour, construction, and a car accident. I soon found myself stalled on the highway. As I scanned the radio looking to be entertained, I heard the following advertisement: "Do you want to be rich? Do you want to be loved? Do you have what it takes to be a Hollywood star?" The ad then shared the phone number for a talent agency. Open auditions were happening the next day.

I imagined my future and saw a red carpet. I suppose that my brain just stopped functioning properly. The boredom of sitting in traffic was overwhelming, and so I called the talent agency. The following day, I found myself in some shady studio auditioning for a ketchup commercial. I will never forget the line I was given to repeat into that high-tech camera: "Heinz 57! Yum, that's good!"

I nailed that line, and I wasn't the least surprised when the phone rang later that afternoon with an offer. "John, we want to work with you. How does two thousand a month sound?" My heart began to pound with excitement, but I decided to play it cool. "I guess that all depends," I said. "How long until the first check arrives in the mail?"

This is where things started spiraling downhill. "Well, Mr. Newton, I suppose that all depends. How quickly can you put a check in the mail?" I felt so awkward and embarrassed, but before hanging up I had to ask. "I thought that actors worked on commission. Why do I have to pay you?" Their response? "I am so sorry to tell you this," they said, "but you are a really bad actor."

Jesus also had a talent for spotting bad actors. A group of Pharisees once approached Jesus and acted like they were among his supporters. "We know that you show deference to no one," they said, "and that your teachings are in accordance with truth." Then they drop the bomb they think will do Jesus in: "Should we pay taxes to Caesar, or shouldn't we?"[17]

They intend to put Jesus in a serious double bind. If Jesus says "yes," he will isolate his fellow Jews who are weighed down by the heavy yoke of Roman rule. However, if Jesus urges his followers to refrain from paying taxes to the emperor, the Romans will

---

17. The NRSV translation uses the word *emperor* and not *Caesar*.

arrest Jesus as a rebel. Aware of their false intentions, Jesus calls them out for putting on a show. "You hypocrites," Jesus says, "why are you putting me to the test?"

Hypocrite has become somewhat of a nasty word in our culture, but this was not the case when Jesus first used the word to describe the behavior of the Pharisees. Jesus was simply using a metaphor that his audience would have been familiar with.[18] The Greek word we translate as "hypocrite" means "actor" in the original Greek. A hypocrite was someone who pretended to be someone else. A hypocrite lived his life on the stage and wore a lot of different masks. Hence when the Pharisees approach Jesus pretending to be on his side, Jesus sees right through their mask. "You are hypocrites," Jesus says, and bad actors to boot.

We know what it is like to put on a mask in the company of others. We want to be loved, and deep down we fear that if our real self were exposed that love and acceptance would be denied to us. We fear rejection and the possibility of being cast out. We learn at a very early age to hide aspects of our self that others might not want us to put forward, and we perfect an image to display to the world. This image is our mask, and sadly so much of growing up is about learning how to perfect this image and about choosing the adult "mask" that works for us.

Our mask can be anything—confidence, wit, intelligence, a clergy collar, a job, a felt sense of religious superiority, or some title. Anything can become our mask, something we use to hide our true self and what we really feel, think, and believe from the world. I don't mean that things like wit, confidence, and titles are necessarily bad. They can be real gifts and aspects of who we are at our core, not to mention a part of our divine vocation. However, authentic easy-yoked discipleship becomes impossible when we confuse the mask we wear with the redeemed self in Christ that we are right now.

---

18. Technically speaking, the author of Matthew's Gospel used a familiar metaphor. Jesus spoke Aramaic, not Greek.

When we invest a lot of time and energy pretending to be someone else, we easily forget who we are in the process. Life becomes a game of hide-and-seek. We hide who we really are, and we seek whatever mask will win us the respect, approval, or support of those whose approval we crave. We live life on the stage and, typically speaking, we are bad actors.

I find myself both encouraged and frightened that Jesus is so capable at seeing through people. Jesus never sees our masks. Jesus always sees us, and Jesus always loves what he sees. Seen in this light, Jesus's response to the Pharisees is not harsh but deeply loving. "Give therefore to the emperor the things that are the emperor's, and to God the things that are God's," he says. A better translation of the Greek word translated "give" (Ἀπόδοτε) is "give back" or "restore." Seeing the emperor's image imprinted on the coin, Jesus wisely responds: "This coin belongs to the emperor, and so give it back to Caesar." Jesus looks through the Pharisees' mask and sees the image of God imprinted on their soul. "You belong to God. Be restored to God. Give yourself back to God." Christians have a word for this process whereby we give ourselves back to God. We call it repentance.

Repentance happens when we give back to God that which is God's—all our heart, mind, soul, and strength (see Luke 10:27). This is not something that we do just once. We repent daily, moment by moment even. We take off the mask and we discover that God cherishes and delights in who we are now and not in the person we hope to become one day.

Repentance has nothing to do with feeling bad for our sins. We call feeling bad about our behavior guilt, and we believe that God has removed our guilt once and for all.[19] Repentance is the

---

19. There is a sense in which the feeling of guilt (as opposed to shame) can be healthy, such as when we observe a gap in our behavior and the values we espouse. But this guilt is meant to be fleeting and to help us learn and grow. If the guilt lasts for more than forty-five minutes, it is probably a neurotic exercise.

giving back of our full self to God at every moment of every day. It is not the first mile in a long march to improvement, but a joyful acknowledgment that we don't have to improve an iota for God's reckless love to flow through our life and into the world.

When I look at my life, I sometimes wonder: do I love God so much that I sometimes forget about my mask? Or do I love my mask so much that I routinely forget about God? Our life is not meant to revolve around perfecting an image that is seen only on the outside. Rather, abundant life is a creative response to grace that leaves God's image perfected on the inside.

There is a divine image imprinted in the depth of your soul. God sees that image—Christ in you, and you in Christ—and God loves what God sees. Give, therefore, to the emperor what belongs to the emperor. But give back to God that which is God's: *you.*

Discussion Questions

1. What masks do you sometimes find yourself wearing? Do you ever have a hard time knowing the difference between the mask and the person wearing the mask?
2. What does the word repentance mean to you? What is the difference between repentance and feeling guilty?
3. Do you believe that Jesus sees everything about you? If so, does this fill you with hope? Why or why not?

Chapter 9

Character

Now when the Pharisees and some of the scribes who had come from Jerusalem gathered around him, they noticed that some of his disciples were eating with defiled hands, that is, without washing them. (For the Pharisees, and all the Jews, do not eat unless they thoroughly wash their hands, thus observing the tradition of the elders; and they do not eat anything from the market unless they wash it; and there are also many other traditions that they observe, the washing of cups, pots, and bronze kettles.) So the Pharisees and the scribes asked him, "Why do your disciples not live according to the tradition of the elders, but eat with defiled hands?" He said to them, "Isaiah prophesied rightly about you hypocrites, as it is written, 'This people honors me with their lips, but their hearts are far from me; in vain do they worship me, teaching human precepts as doctrines.' You abandon the commandment of God and hold to human tradition." Then he called the crowd again and said to them, "Listen to me, all of you, and understand: there is nothing outside a person that by going in can defile, but the things that come out are what defile. For it is from within, from the human heart, that evil intentions come: fornication, theft, murder, adultery, avarice, wickedness, deceit, licentiousness, envy, slander, pride, folly. All these evil things come from within, and they defile a person." (Mark 7:1–8, 14–15, 21–23)

I recently received an e-mail with the following subject line: "You might be an Episcopalian if . . ." Allow me to share a few highlights from this semi-humorous piece of spam.

> You might be an Episcopalian if, when watching Star Wars and hearing "May the Force be with you," you automatically reply, "And also with you!"
> You might be an Episcopalian if, when approaching a row of seats at a movie theatre, you genuflect before entering.
> You might be an Episcopalian if, while looking for a can opener in the church kitchen, all you can find are corkscrews.

On and on went the jokes about how only Episcopalians understand that a senior warden does not work at the local prison, that a Primate is not a monkey, and that the *sursum corda* is not a surgical procedure. "How many Episcopalians does it take to change a light bulb?" Answer: why would we ever want to *change*?

This e-mail was poking fun at a universal phenomenon, namely that we all participate in groups with very specific identity markers. Sociologically speaking, all groups adopt identity markers: certain ways of speaking, behaving, dressing, and acting that serve to distinguish insiders from outsiders. For instance, if I encounter a person with dark lipstick, black clothes, dark makeup, and multiple piercings, I would venture to guess that he or she is part of America's gothic subculture and not a United States senator.

Religious groups always seem to be the most passionate about their identity markers. As an Episcopal priest, I love our identity markers. Our Book of Common Prayer, the liturgy, and the Daily Office have been means through which I have come to know and love Jesus Christ. Identity markers are not inherently bad or wrong, but they always go wrong if they make us feel superior to other groups. We no longer see ourselves as different, but better.

Jesus and the Pharisees frequently debated what identity markers were important and which ones were not. Like all first-century Jews, the Pharisees believed that God had chosen them to be different. The word *holy* means "separate," and the Pharisees understood that God had given the people of Israel a clear command: "be holy, for I the LORD your God am holy" (Lev. 20:26). God, it seemed, was a Different-Sort-of-Being altogether and, as God's chosen people, Israel had a divine calling to be different. But *how so?*

The Pharisees answered this question primarily in terms of ritual purity. The Pharisees had strict ways of living, cooking, and eating that made them different from non-Jews. These purity laws were important to the Pharisees. As an occupied people ruled by the Roman state, the Pharisees felt as if their identity was under attack and in constant need of being defended. The purity code was the Pharisees' way of differentiating themselves from the outside world. They deeply feared being assimilated into the Greco-Roman culture that increasingly gripped people's minds, imaginations, and hearts. The purity code was an identity marker that allowed the Pharisees to say to the world: "We are Jews. We are different. We do not live like the rest of the world."

I understand why the Pharisees had such a difficult time with Jesus. Jesus seemed to be constantly taking something that marked out his own people as different only to deem it as completely irrelevant. Jesus healed on the Sabbath, touched the unclean, spoke to women in public, welcomed children, and often took people away from their families. Jesus was an iconoclast with respect to conventional religious practice. This makes me wonder: is Jesus saying that identity markers are not

important, or is Jesus critiquing the Pharisees and us for sometimes making the wrong identity markers important?

Jesus wants his disciples to be different because of God's
presence in their lives. However, I somehow just can't believe that
traditional ways that Christians have differentiated themselves
from the culture—moral purity, style of worship, stances on
certain political issues, and so on—matter much to Jesus at all.
Jesus's chief concern is always with the human heart. "Nothing
outside can defile a person by going in," he said. "For it is from
within," Jesus taught, "that emerges all the mess that ends up
messing up our world. The inner spiritual gunk is always what
defiles people, families, culture, and the world."

Jesus knows how we tend to trust in externals that make
us feel superior to everyone else and that really we are all the
same on the inside. All people—priests, prostitutes, Democrats,
Republicans, prison guards, prisoners, and presidents—have the
same inner gunk. There is no light coming from the bulb, and
Jesus wants to change it and give us a new one.

Jesus emphasized the importance of *internal* identity markers,
and not external ones. The purity laws of the Hebrew Scriptures
were always meant to point to a deeper purity of the heart.

There is a saying that has become popular in our culture: "Just do what is in your heart." I don't think Jesus would
endorse this. Not everything in our heart is good or useful to
the betterment of society. There is a real self-righteousness
within the human heart that does not want to die. There is
a part of us not bothered when certain groups are excluded.
We feel special when we are on the inside and someone else is
on the outside. Self-righteousness lives deep within the human
heart, and that is why our hearts must change. We need a new
bulb. Light doesn't always shine as brightly from the old one as
we think.

Jesus wants his disciples to be different, and as I see it we only
have two options. On the one hand, we can make our faith primarily about external identity markers. In a scary and confusing

world, we can anxiously cling to artificial ways of distinguishing ourselves from them—whoever "them" happens to be. We can also give Christ our heart and say, "Take all of it. I want to change. I need to change." We can be grateful for our external identity markers, but also hold them a bit lighter. We can acknowledge that they are temporary and that they are only valuable to the extent that God uses them to transform our heart. It is always this commitment to transformation, to a new bulb, that Jesus prays would capture his disciples' imaginations. There is a name for this renovation of the heart: character.

Character is not about being better than everyone else. In fact, character is grounded in a deep understanding that we are just like everyone else—deeply flawed, and yet loved to our core. Character is a forgetting of the self, a desire to find grace in all moments and people, and a passion to include more and more people in God's ever-widening circle of reconciliation and love that flows from the cross. This spiritual posture will not make you better than anyone, but it will certainly differentiate you from our performance-driven world.

Jesus himself was unique in that his focus was on the formation of our character, or the "inner man" as Paul would sometimes say (Rom. 7:22; 2 Cor. 4:16). I dream one day I will get a "You might be a Christian if . . ." e-mail that has more substance than jokes about corkscrews and liturgical idiosyncrasies. Such an e-mail might read: you might be a Christian if you are known for your soft heart, if your compassion for rich and poor alike causes you pain, if forgiveness is a daily practice, if joy is a hallmark of your life, and if people are routinely drawn to your warmth, understanding, and perspective that all of life is a gift.

Jesus was committed to a different way of being different. It is a way of being different that excludes no one, except perhaps party-poopers who are allergic to grace and forgiveness. The irony, of course, is Jesus's way of being different is grounded in a wonderfully wild and hilarious paradox: on the inside, we are all the same.

Discussion Questions

1. What external identity markers do you associate with your church, denomination, or faith community? What does it mean to honor these identity markers without clinging to them?
2. What does the word character mean to you? How do we become a person of character?
3. In what sense are Jesus's disciples called to be different from non-Christians? In what sense will Jesus's disciples never be different from non-Christians?

Chapter 10

Evangelism

Once while Jesus was standing beside the lake of Gennesaret, and the crowd was pressing in on him to hear the word of God, he saw two boats there at the shore of the lake; the fishermen had gone out of them and were washing their nets. He got into one of the boats, the one belonging to Simon, and asked him to put out a little way from the shore. Then he sat down and taught the crowds from the boat. When he had finished speaking, he said to Simon, "Put out into the deep water and let down your nets for a catch." Simon answered, "Master, we have worked all night long but have caught nothing. Yet if you say so, I will let down the nets." When they had done this, they caught so many fish that their nets were beginning to break. So they signaled to their partners in the other boat to come and help them. And they came and filled both boats, so that they began to sink. But when Simon Peter saw it, he fell down at Jesus's knees, saying, "Go away from me, Lord, for I am a sinful man!" For he and all who were with him were amazed at the catch of fish that they had taken; and so also were James and John, sons of Zebedee, who were partners with Simon.

> Then Jesus said to Simon, "Do not be afraid; from now on
> you will be catching people." (Luke 5:1–10)

I have a love-hate relationship with catchy church signs. I love them because they are catchy, but I also hate them because they are catchy. Consider the following real advertisements that churches have put on a sign hoping to "catch" people driving by the church property:

> "Free coffee and everlasting life:
> membership has its privileges!"

> "Don't let worries kill you: let the church help!"

> "Looking for a lifeguard? Ours walks on water."

These signs are marketing tools meant to grab people's attention, hook them, and get them to come inside the sanctuary. Marketing is all about catching people. As a business major in college, I recall reading an article that compared effective marketing to a highly contagious virus. Good marketing seeps into our minds and hearts so strongly that we can't help but transmit the message to others, who then transmit it to others, and so on until the ad reaches millions. Good marketing will always catch more people than you ever could have imagined initially, or as the article put it, "a catch beyond your wildest dreams."

This makes me ponder Jesus's promise to Simon Peter: "From now on you will be catching people." It is among my favorite verses in scripture because it reminds me that evangelism is at the heart of the Christian faith. As the Book of Common Prayer puts it, our chief ministry is to "represent Christ and his Church" and to "bear witness to him wherever [we] may be" (BCP, 855). *Wherever* we may be—at home, the office, the grocery store, the gym, a bar, with friends—God desires that our presence bear witness to Jesus. We get that somehow we are supposed to be catching people. It is the *how* that we struggle with.

God doesn't want us to catch people through any sort of typical marketing scheme. There may be room for traditional forms of advertising every now and again, but we are lying to ourselves if we think that solid marketing will grow the church. People in our world are sick and tired of being sold things all day long, and I can't help but wonder if seekers sometimes feel like they are being sold Jesus when they visit our churches.

We sometimes talk about the church as if it were the latest technological gadget. We point out all the benefits that come with joining our congregation—the children's ministry, the outreach we do in the community, the sense of peace and connection we feel—and before you know it we find ourselves describing a product and not a person. Offering great spiritual products is not our mission. People are not looking for a product. They are looking for a person—and that person is God.

People sometimes call the gospel passage quoted above the "call of the first disciples," but that is a complete misnomer. Luke's version of this account isn't a call story, but a pronouncement story. Jesus does not call Simon Peter. He announces to Simon what he will now do with the rest of his life—not fishing, but catching. "From now on you will be catching people."

The Greek word translated "catch" is found only in Luke's Gospel. It's a compound word that is more accurately translated "catch alive" or "capture alive."[20] It also meant to revive or to restore life to something—to capture it to make it come alive, or to catch something with the express purpose of infusing it with new life. Perhaps the best modern translation of ζωγρῶν isn't *catch* but *captivate*, which means to attract with beauty and excellence. "Don't be afraid, Simon," Jesus says. "From now on you will be *captivating* people."

This may sound like a funny thing for Jesus to say to Simon Peter, but I think it would have made sense to Peter. Jesus had

---

20. The Greek word translated "catch" is ζωγρῶν.

already captivated Peter himself. In the context of Luke's Gospel, Jesus has just left Simon's house, where his mother-in-law was sick with a fever. Jesus entered her house and healed her, revived her, and infused her with new life, and Peter had a front row seat for the whole episode.

I can't help but think that in that moment Peter was utterly captivated by Jesus, or completely "sold," as marketing folk sometimes say. In fact, before Jesus and Peter even had the chance to leave the house, all kinds of people were brought to Jesus—the sick, the unclean, the demon-possessed, the broken-hearted, and people on the fringes—and without fail, Jesus infused new life into every single one of them.

Simon Peter got to witness firsthand the beauty and excellence of a rabbi with an easy yoke who brings life to everyone he meets. Peter has already been caught. Sure, he tries to wriggle away and jump out of the net. "Go away from me, Lord," he says, "for I am a sinful man." But Jesus won't allow it. "Sorry, Peter, you have been caught, and from now on you will be catching people, too."

The question we must ask ourselves if we wish to make a love-spreading difference in our world is: have *we* been caught by the love of Christ? Do we know, firsthand, the beauty and excellence of this captivating Lord who brings life to everyone he encounters? Do we understand that even if we tell Jesus to leave like Peter did, Jesus's answer will always be no?

When our life is caught up in the kingdom of God, catching others for God's kingdom is just what happens. Like a highly contagious virus, being caught in the kingdom affects people so strongly they transmit it to others, who then convey it to others, continuously passing Christ's love until it has reached the whole world.

Marketing and sales schemes can take us only so far. We only truly catch people when we ourselves have been caught and when we learn to love others with the same reckless abandon with which Christ loves us. This is *how* we are to evangelize the world. We are to captivate people with the love of Christ and to capture them in a way that infuses them with fresh life.

Please don't ask the tired, old question: how do we get more people to come to our church? Try this question on instead. How do we as a faith community become so enamored, so caught up in Christ, so committed to the work of God's kingdom, that we become living and breathing signs of grace?

Whether people realize it or not, they're not looking for a product. They're looking for a person—for the One who created them, who loves them, and who has the power to infuse them with life. "We wish to see Jesus" is our world's unconscious cry.[21] If being captured by Jesus's love becomes the goal of our lives and our mission as a church, and if we look to Jesus daily to be infused with fresh life, our lives will become bait that catches people for the kingdom of God. That's not a call or an invitation, but a pronouncement. Caught people always catch people—a bounty beyond our wildest dreams.

Discussion Questions

1. What do you see as the primary difference between evangelism and marketing? Which of the two requires more creativity? More vulnerability?
2. Have you been "caught" by Christ's love? If so, was this a one-time experience or more of a process over time?
3. Do you believe that evangelism is essential to the mission of the church? Why or why not?

---

21. See John 12:21.

Chapter 11

Compassion

The apostles gathered around Jesus, and told him all that they had done and taught. He said to them, "Come away to a deserted place all by yourselves and rest a while." For many were coming and going, and they had no leisure even to eat. And they went away in the boat to a deserted place by themselves. Now many saw them going and recognized them, and they hurried there on foot from all the towns and arrived ahead of them. As he went ashore, he saw a great crowd; and he had compassion for them, because they were like sheep without a shepherd; and he began to teach them many things. When they had crossed over, they came to land at Gennesaret and moored the boat. When they got out of the boat, people at once recognized him, and rushed about that whole region and began to bring the sick on mats to wherever they heard he was. And wherever he went, into villages or cities or farms, they laid the sick in the marketplaces, and begged him that they might touch even the fringe of his cloak; and all who touched it were healed. (Mark 6:30–34, 53–56)

People sometimes assume that members of the clergy are a spiritually superior subsection of humankind. They do not think that we have neuroses or that we wrestle with insecurity like other mere mortals. People who make these assumptions probably don't *know* their minister very well. They may admire her sermons or feel comforted by his pastoral presence, but anyone who knows a member of the clergy understands that we wrestle with our faith like everyone else. In our teaching and preaching, we articulate our own felt need for salvation and grace—if the congregation happens to "catch" a few crumbs of grace along the way, even better.

Few clergy can acknowledge this truth, and our interactions with one another are not always "full of grace and truth" (John 1:14). When we gather for some big event like our annual clergy conference or diocesan convention, we have limited time to catch up and so we default to our standard question: how are things going at the church?

I have noticed tremendous pressure to give what seems to be the only acceptable answer to this question: *busy.* "Things are busy," we say in our most exhausted voice, doing our best to sound important. "Busy, busy, busy!"

This response serves as the cue for whoever asked us the question to tell us how busy they are, too. I wish I could say that I refuse to participate in this game, but I am the chief sinner. Even if I am not busy, when people ask me about my ministry I never fail to give the impression that I have too many plates spinning, as if exhaustion were a point of pride.

My friend Bert often reminds me that when someone tells you how busy they are, what they really want to communicate is how *important* they are. Our desire for others to perceive us as busy and our desire to feel important go hand in hand. Brené Brown argues that what makes American culture unique is that exhaustion is a status symbol. According to Brown, "We are a nation of exhausted and overstressed adults raising overscheduled children. We think accomplishments . . . will bring joy and meaning, but that pursuit could be the very thing that's keeping us so tired and afraid to slow down."[22] Brown's point is that it can feel scary to slow down because a part of us believes that who we are is tied to what we *do* and that a significant life is a busy life.

Life can be hectic, and there are seasons in life when survival really is the goal. If we are caring for young children or working three jobs to keep the lights on, we may need to work nonstop. God is fully with us in these busy seasons. Life situations often force many to juggle a lot. I do not question being busy, only our desire for people to think that we are busy. I question when we become apologetic and sheepish for taking all our vacation days and for getting nine hours of sleep.

Outer busyness cannot block God's reckless love. The loud churnings of inner busyness alone deafen us to the still, small voice of God. When inner busyness takes over, we feel that who we are and what we contribute is not enough. We are haunted by the thought that God, the universe, or our parents expect more from us. We fearfully move at a frantic pace to stay ahead of that shameful voice that insists that we need to prove ourselves.

When members of the clergy, that is, Jesus's apostles, gather around Jesus to brag about how busy they are, Jesus does not condemn his disciples, nor does he reinforce their frantic pace with false encouragement. Instead, Jesus smiles, takes a deep breath, invites them to rest, and reminds them that they need to eat. "Come away to a deserted place all by yourselves," he says, "and rest a while."

I wonder: have *you* heard Jesus give you permission to drop whatever inner burdens and fears you are carrying and to rest in the grace of God's compassion?

---

22. Brené Brown, *Gifts of Imperfection: Let Go of Who You Think You're Supposed to Be and Embrace Who You Are* (Center City, MN: Hazelden, 2010), 102.

A wise person once told me there is only one basic theological question that matters: how does your God view the world? In other words, do you believe that God is threatening, vengeful, angry, or vindictive? Is God approachable, and if so, under what conditions? If we are morally pure? Through a carefully guarded ritual supervised by a priest?

How does your God view the world? This is the basic theological question and the second is like unto it: how does your God view *you*? Get these two questions right and you will get *life* right. Everything else is just commentary and footnotes.

The Bible gives a life-changing answer to this question by insisting that the God revealed in Jesus Christ views the world and all of us with boundless compassion. Jesus's compassion is what made him such an attractive person. Unlike the heavy-yoked rabbis of Jesus's day, people did not have to worry whether they were pure enough or spiritually healthy enough in Jesus's presence. When people were with Jesus, he made them feel like they were *enough*.

In a busy, performance-driven world, I find that I need to return to this grace-soaked ground of Christ's compassion daily. God's boundless compassion for humanity is the best news in the world. It is the reason prostitutes broke into people's homes to kiss Jesus's feet and why lepers flocked to Jesus expecting to be touched. Compassion is why people too sick to walk were dragged to Jesus on mats. Just about everyone knew, except perhaps for the disciples, that Jesus was the most compassionate man alive. Jesus's compassion, and not his teaching, wisdom, knowledge of the Torah, or even his miraculous powers to heal, made and makes him such an attractive person.

How does your God view the world?

Only when we know God has boundless compassion for us can we lay our burdens at Jesus's feet and give ourselves a break, not to mention give other people a break. The moment we confess that God views the whole world with boundless compassion we will start to see ourselves as the recipients of God's compassion, and we always give that which we receive.

I chuckle when people read the Bible and see Jesus interacting with people who struggle only to point out how much Jesus loves the marginalized, beaten-up people in our world as if they were *someone else*. When we read the Bible in this way, we conclude that we are strong, they are weak, and that our job is to serve the less fortunate.

Reading the Bible in this way is not altogether untrue, but it certainly is convenient. It allows us to see ourselves as different and privileged, a slightly superior subsection of humans. In this view of the world, we are the missionaries and they are the mission field. We are the Body of Christ, the people with the balm, and the marginalized others are the ones in need of healing.

A myth we often perpetuate is that the first task of a Christian is to extend compassion to others. That sounds nice and holy, like something a religious person should say, but it's just not possible. We can only give to someone that which we have received. Easy-yoked discipleship is first and foremost about waking up to see that *we* are the lepers, prostitutes, prisoners, demon-possessed, diseased, unclean, lame, and sick for whom Christ died. We are the recipients of God's boundless compassion, and what we receive we *always* give to others.

People are exhausted, and they are looking for permission to drop their burdens. We want a community of grace where our soul can find rest and where the demons of fear and shame cannot survive. Busy churches and busy people cannot minister to such a hurting world, only people who have entered God's rest.

"Come away to a deserted place all by yourselves," Jesus says, "and rest a while." In that place of rest, you will find boundless compassion. As we receive, we give; and in learning to rest, we find ourselves engaged in God's work, perhaps for the very first time.

Discussion Questions

1. Do you ever find yourself wanting others to perceive you as being busier than you are? If so, why?
2. Jesus invites his disciples to "rest." What is the difference between rest and leisure? Do you believe that rest is a spiritual practice? Why or why not?
3. Do you believe that God views all people with boundless compassion? Who do you often struggle to feel compassion for?

Chapter 12

Joy

As the Father has loved me, so I have loved you; abide in my love. If you keep my commandments, you will abide in my love, just as I have kept my Father's commandments and abide in his love. I have said these things to you so that my joy may be in you, and that your joy may be complete. (John 15:9–11)

Every year my friend Edward hosts a Halloween party at his house. I don't get too enthused about costumes, and I am not good at picking out things to wear. As a priest, I wear a uniform, which is fine with me because I am not a creative or trendy dresser. I have worn the same Halloween costume for the past seven years. I bought a mad scientist costume in 2011 for $29.99 and I haven't looked back since.

Last year, one of my friends dressed up as a Puritan. She wore no makeup, no flashy clothes, but most importantly she did not smile or laugh the entire night. Her goal was to look completely joyless.

Her costume was somewhat of a caricature, though I concede that Puritans did not have a reputation for being the life of the party. Some Puritans believed that laughter was evil. I heard that the Puritans sentenced one man to three days in jail for smiling at his baptism. Apparently, they thought that following Jesus was serious business and that God expects us to frown in this life to secure a smile in the next life.

We are heirs to this "Christianity-is-serious-business" philosophy. We often assume that discipleship is about doing our moral duty. Good Christians, we think, roll up their sleeves, stuff the deepest desires of their heart, and dedicate their life to a divine purpose at significant cost to themselves.

This conflating of discipleship with moral duty sounds nice and pious, but the Christianity-is-serious-business worldview doesn't mesh with Jesus's easy-yoked gospel of reckless love: "I have said these things to you so that my joy may be in you, and that your joy may be complete." Joy is an unmistakable mark of the presence of God's Holy Spirit (see Gal. 5:22). Life in Christ is above all else a life of deep and abiding joy.

In our performance-driven world of anxiety and fear, living a joy-filled life can be a challenge. Deep joy is nearly impossible when we are preoccupied with things or attached to external circumstances. Psalm 1 compares the joy-filled person to a tree that is planted by streams of water. This psalm draws a distinction between a tree with roots that run deep into a nearby stream and a tree that depends on the fickleness of the outside rain for nourishment. It highlights the difference between drawing on inner resources, an intimate relationship with God, and depending on outside factors to make us feel happy and secure.

What is the difference between happiness and joy? Joy is always available to us in the present moment and stems from an awareness of God's reckless love. Happiness, on the other hand, depends on some external state of events that our mind projects into the future. There is usually a "when" and a "then" that precedes happiness. *When* I get the promotion, or pay off my debt, or publish this book, or get this person to validate me, *then* I will be happy. The irony, of course, is that this when-and-then mentality is what fuels our deep unhappiness. It blinds us to the joy that belongs to us in Christ Jesus right now, in the present moment.

Living a joy-filled life is impossible if we are always trying to get rid of things in our life that hurt or feel unpleasant. We get rid of our boredom and anxiety by seeking distractions. We get rid of our insecurity by eliminating risks. We get rid of our disappointment by downplaying our deepest hopes. All the while, we forget the major paradox of the Christian gospel; joy is not found in avoiding our cross, but rather in embracing our unique share with Jesus and the cross for the sake of the world. "Suffering produces endurance, and endurance produces character, and character produces hope" (Rom. 5:3–4).

I don't mean to say that pain is good. I simply wish to remind our deepest self that God is goodness itself; redemption is precisely what happens when God's reckless love moves us deeper into our pain in such a way that we more accurately mirror Christ to the world. This capacity to mirror Christ, to *know* Him, completes our joy. There is no lasting joy in our ideas about Christ, only in our *knowledge* of Christ.

God desires joy to infuse the life of every human being. I cannot give you a recipe for growing in joy. Joy is not a strategy but the very life of God. Joy is not something we possess, but rather our God who possesses us in what Richard Rohr calls "the naked now." We catch joy from our Creator in the present moment. That is why it is impossible to be joyful later. God only offers us joy, the life of Christ, now.

God is the most joy-filled being in the entire universe. When God created the heavens and the earth, God did not casually remark, "That'll have to do." Rather, God screamed, "VERY GOOD" over the whole creation. God does not create out of necessity, but rather from a sense of pure and overflowing joy. Joy is foundational to the heart of God.

Jesus is the incarnation, the embodiment and physical manifestation, of our joy-filled God. Obedience to Jesus was never meant to rob us of joy. On the contrary, keeping Jesus's commandments and abiding in his love are what make our joy complete. As the late theologian and hymn writer John Newton put it:

> Our pleasure and our duty,
> Though opposite before,
> Since we have seen His beauty,
> Are joined to part no more:
> It is our highest pleasure,
> No less than duty's call,
> To love Him beyond measure,
> And serve Him with our all.[23]

In my writing, teaching, and preaching, I aim to be descriptive, as opposed to being prescriptive. I wish to describe God's reckless love and not prescribe behaviors and practices that we can do to draw closer to God. I don't like telling people what they "should" do, mainly because it doesn't work. Everyone, it seems, is haunted by what they should be doing in our performance-driven world. Our list of "shoulds" makes us feel miserable, and we offload that misery onto everyone around us. *Should* is one of my least favorite words.

However, from time to time I do break my own rules. After all, to say, "You should never tell people what they should do" is a funny trap that folk like me who want to prioritize grace sometimes fall into. Thus, I will offer one prescription.

You should celebrate right now.

Allow the Spirit to draw you outside of yourself. Dance. Sing. Be goofy. Live. Love. Lighten up. Right now. Christ has died, Christ has risen, Christ will come again (even though Christ never left and was mysteriously here before he came). God has won, will win, and wins right now. You are free now. Celebrate. You really should.

---

23. https://davidshane.blog/2011/07/17/john-newton-wrote-other-hymns/ (accessed September 19, 2017).

God built human beings to celebrate. We are made in the image of the Trinity, the one-big-celebration we call God.

I think back to my friend's Halloween costume. There is nothing scarier or more frightening than a person who never smiles and laughs. Nothing is scarier than a person utterly lacking in joy, especially when their joylessness is rooted in religious observance and done in the name of Jesus. Christians, of all people, should be the life of the party that's happening on earth.

God's reckless love is flowing into your life right now. It may be well disguised, like treasure hidden in a field. But you are that field. Find the treasure, and your joy will be complete.

Discussion Questions

1. Do you believe that there is a difference between happiness and joy? If so, what? Have you ever experienced joy when you were unhappy, or happiness when you felt no joy?
2. Do you believe that God is the most joy-filled being in the entire universe? What do you imagine God was doing before the creation of the universe?
3. Do you think Jesus was a "serious" person? Why or why not? Do you think that Christians are called to take their faith "seriously"?

Chapter 13

Reconciliation

What do you think? If a shepherd has a hundred sheep, and one of them has gone astray, does he not leave the ninety-nine on the mountains and go in search of the one that went astray? And if he finds it, truly I tell you, he rejoices over it more than over the ninety-nine that never went astray. So it is not the will of your Father in heaven that one of these little ones should be lost. If another member of the church sins against you, go and point out the fault when the two of you are alone. If the member listens to you, you have regained that one. (Matt. 18:12–15)

What scandalizes you? What do you find to be so immoral and offensive that you are shocked whenever you see it?

All the juicy scandals, both in our culture and in the church, involve money and/or sex. I find that religious folk are more easily scandalized than others. I know a few fundamentalists who are scandalized by smoking, drinking, and reality television. I know a few Episcopalians who are scandalized by fundamentalists. When my dad worships with my daughter at the kid-friendly, contemporary service, he never fails to mention how appalled he is that a special pipe organ can't be installed in the gymnasium where we worship. All sorts of things offend people. What scandalizes you?

None of the traditional juicy scandals seemed to bother Jesus. Jesus was accused of being a drunkard, or a "winebibber" as the King James Version puts it. He also routinely sought the company of all kinds of outcasts. It's not that Jesus loved sin, but clearly, financial swindling, alcohol, religious impurity, and sex didn't horrify him.

Jesus was outraged by broken relationships and by our unwillingness to forgive one another. Jesus hated the chronic enmity that so often characterizes human relationships and our complacency with respect to mending those relationships. Jesus taught that all the law and prophets could be reduced to a single command: love God, love other people, and love our self. Our lack of love scandalized Jesus more than anything else.

Love does not come easily. Love is costly, as love always requires sacrifice. It is much easier to be polite, polished, and proper than it is to recklessly sacrifice our wants and wishes to bless and build up another human being. I can scarcely offer my loved ones the same reckless forgiveness and grace that God offers me, not to mention the people I find irritating.

People hurt us, and we hurt people. In Matthew 18, Jesus begins his teaching by saying "*if* another member of the church sins against you," but Jesus could easily have begun that sentence with the word *when*. Human beings hurt other human beings. This is not a question of if, but when.

Hurting people and being hurt is inevitable. Jesus is not offended that we hurt one another per se. The scandal, in God's mind, is that we hold on to our hurts and refuse to extend forgiveness. Jesus routinely taught that nothing threatened our standing with God more than a lack of forgiveness. "Go," Jesus pleads with his disciples. "Make the first move. Do whatever it takes to regain your brother and sister."

Jesus understands human brokenness, and putting broken relationships back together is God's favorite cup of tea. Jesus mends our relationship with God, and then he mends our relationship with each other. This mending of our relationship with God and one another is called reconciliation. Reconciliation is an accomplished fact, a cosmic reality, whether we see it or not. "It is finished" (see John 19:30).

God sees all relationships as reconciled *now* in his Son Jesus Christ, the Incarnate Word, the second person of the Trinity. As such, human brokenness is not a scandal. If anything, broken relationships are a mere misunderstanding—a failure on our part to see what God sees and a corresponding inability to go with the flow of God's new creation. The scandal, from Jesus's point of view, is that we can be so oblivious to, detached from, and apathetic toward the broken relationships in our life and that we lack the love to "go" to people who hurt us and seek reconciliation. What outrages Jesus is the possibility that we would ever stop seeking reconciliation, and that we're not as reckless with our forgiveness as God is wild with mercy and compassion toward us.

Every fiber of our being screams out against being the reckless lovers God invites us to be. We are not inclined to take the initiative to repair broken relationships. We hate the vulnerability and blow to our ego that comes with listening to how our behavior contributed to the relational breach. It is so much easier to condemn. As such, we blame. We judge. We allow our anger to fester. We gossip. We slander. We stew. We suffer silently. We fail to love. Sometimes we fight. Sometimes we flee. Sometimes we just cease caring. We will do just about anything to avoid the death to self that always comes with resurrecting love.

Our lack of love is a form of spiritual amnesia. We fail to love and forgive because we forget that God is always loving and forgiving us. God proved that love for us—while we were still sinners Christ died for us (see Romans 5:8). God took the initiative, when we broke God's heart, to become incarnate in the person of Jesus Christ with the single aim of reconciling all human beings to God. God asks us to make the first move as a way of inviting us to share in God's life. In seeking reconciliation, we are only doing that which God always does. "My Father is still working," Jesus says, "and I also am working" (John 5:17). Reconciliation is God's work, and what Jesus essentially says to his disciples is "Come be our partner." Or as Paul so eloquently puts it, "All this is from God, who reconciled us to himself through Christ, and has given us the ministry of reconciliation" (2 Cor. 5:18).

There is nothing practical about a ministry of reconciliation. Jesus likens God to a shepherd who is so impractical, so without regard, that he will leave ninety-nine sheep behind to seek out and save the one sheep that got away. "It is not the will of your Father," Jesus says, "that anyone should be lost, and so if someone sins against you leave the ninety-nine practical reasons behind and restore the sheep that got away."

Reconciliation is not for practical people who value the world's wisdom. God's reckless love means that we fight evil by forgiving it and seek reconciliation with others rather than asking who is to blame. When we shamelessly love other people as God loves us, things get messy. We will be rejected, laughed at, and routinely misunderstood. The world will always call foolish what God calls wise (see 1 Cor. 1:18). But as we recall from chapter one, Jesus Christ was such a fool.

How foolish are we willing to be in our relationships with other people? Do we understand how irrational God is in God's dealings with us? Only a fool would leave ninety-nine sheep behind to save the straggler too obtuse to stay with the pack, and yet Jesus insists that this is precisely the nature of God. Jesus invites us to be fools, too.

Discussion Questions

1. What behaviors do you find to be truly scandalous? Do you think that we should be appalled by such behaviors? Why or why not?

2. Is there a difference between forgiveness and reconciliation? If so, what?

3. Have you experienced reconciliation with an estranged love one? Is there anyone in your life that you are currently estranged from? If so, what prevents you from seeking reconciliation?

Chapter 14

Endurance

"Those who eat my flesh and drink my blood abide in me, and I in them. Just as the living Father sent me, and I live because of the Father, so whoever eats me will live because of me. This is the bread that came down from heaven, not like that which your ancestors ate, and they died. But the one who eats this bread will live forever." He said these things while he was teaching in the synagogue at Capernaum. When many of his disciples heard it, they said, "This teaching is difficult; who can accept it?" But Jesus, being aware that his disciples were complaining about it, said to them, "Does this offend you? Then what if you were to see the Son of Man ascending to where he was before? It is the spirit that gives life; the flesh is useless. The words that I have spoken to you are spirit and life. But among you there are some who do not believe." For Jesus knew from the first who were the ones that did not believe, and who was the one that would betray him. And he said, "For this reason I have told you that no one can come to me unless it is granted by the Father." Because of this many of his disciples turned back and no longer went about with him. So Jesus asked the twelve, "Do you also wish to go away?"

Simon Peter answered him, "Lord, to whom can we go? You have the words of eternal life. We have come to believe and know that you are the Holy One of God." (John 6:56–69)

Sir Ernest Shackleton was a polar explorer who led three expeditions to the Antarctic at the beginning of the twentieth century, each of which was fraught with danger. On one of these expeditions his ship, *Endurance,* got stuck in a pack of ice for almost three years. Miraculously, not one man lost his life. After three years of being stranded, Shackleton and his crew boarded lifeboats and braved the cold and stormy seas for 720 nautical miles. They eventually made their way back to civilization, which had long assumed that the men were all dead.

Shackleton was a good and faithful captain. He clearly cherished a good adventure, and he wasn't stifled by the prospect of danger. Consider the following advertisement that he placed in the newspaper to recruit men for one of his expeditions:

Men wanted for a hazardous journey. Low wages, bitter cold, long hours of complete darkness. Safe return doubtful. Honor and recognition in the event of success.[24]

I love the sheer honesty of these words, and I sometimes use them to contemplate life in Christ. In our conscious choice to follow Jesus, we sign up for a hazardous journey. There are moments of bitter spiritual cold and darkness along the way. We never return from our journey to the safe and comfortable life we knew before.

There may be times in our spiritual life when we are tempted to pack our bags and go home. Faith is not about taking control, but about throwing caution to the wind and braving the stormy seas. As Jesus told his disciples, the point of faith is not to taste Jesus but to swallow him whole. We eat his flesh and drink his

---

24. www.campaignlive.co.uk/article/history-advertising-no-137-sir-ernest-shackletons-men-wanted-ad/1351657 (accessed September 19, 2017).

blood as we scream a wholehearted and trustful "Yes!" to whatever dangerous expedition God has planned for our life.

Endurance is at the heart of the spiritual life. We all face
hard times and confusing moments when life doesn't make
sense. These moments are deeply significant, and they force us
to come face to face with an important choice. Will we walk away,
or will we go all in?

Not all of Jesus's first followers endured to the end. As John's
Gospel puts it, "many of his disciples turned back and no longer went about with him" (John 6:66). In other words, they suc-
cumbed to their confusion and fear, they threw in the towel, and
they walked away. The journey felt too hazardous and scary.

This was clearly not true for all the disciples. Peter sticks with
Jesus, as do the other apostles who follow Peter's lead. Peter's
faithfulness is delightfully surprising. Peter was far from perfect.
Peter tried to convince Jesus that dying on a cross was a bad idea
and denied knowing Jesus three times on the toughest night of
Jesus's life.

Peter may not always exude integrity and understanding, but
what Peter does display is the only thing Jesus wants. *Peter stays.*
When the others are tired, confused, offended, and confounded
by Jesus's words about eating his flesh and drinking his blood,
Peter sticks by Jesus's side. Peter has embraced the hazardous
adventure that is life in Christ. Peter's words are both an inspira-
tion and a challenge to us who often struggle to endure in our
walk with Christ. I paraphrase:

> Lord, to whom can we go? Do we understand your teach-
> ing? No, we do not. Are we slightly offended by your words?
> Yes, we are. However, we have come to know and believe
> that you are the Holy One of God. Therefore, I speak on
> behalf of the twelve. We are all in. Lord, to whom else can
> we go? Let the expedition continue!

I want to cultivate a faith that deep and committed in my
own life, a faith that can endure when the floods come and the

wind blows (see Matt. 7:25). After all, Jesus did not say "the one who exhibits perfection" shall be saved but "the one who *endures* to the end will be saved" (Matt. 24:13).

Endurance is impossible unless we are willing to be vulnerable. A sustainable faith requires that we be honest: with God, with ourselves, and with each other. We cannot pretend to be stronger, smarter, holier, or more put-together than we are. Peter had zero qualms about admitting that he was deeply confused and even slightly troubled by Jesus's teaching. Peter was vulnerable and honest with Jesus.

When we are not being vulnerable in our spiritual life, faith often feels like we are just mechanically going through the motions. We give God a few Sunday mornings a month and perhaps a small fraction of our income, but we miss out on a vulnerable intimacy with Jesus. Vulnerability requires naming those places in our life where we feel scared, confused, and inadequate. Like Peter, we give Jesus our confusion. "Lord," we say, "I don't understand why terrible things happen in our world or why you would allow oppression to continue. I don't understand why I am so scared of death, and why feelings of unworthiness still haunt me even today. But, I love you Jesus, and I trust you. To whom else can I go?" This is vulnerability. We admit that there are seasons in this expedition we call life that feel dark and scary, and we cling to Jesus and to one another during that experience.

Endurance also requires clarity that Jesus is our captain amidst life's storms. This side of eternity, some questions just don't have adequate answers. We can embrace the vulnerability of that reality and lean on Jesus when confronted with life's mysteries, or we can complain, grow bitter, and walk away as some of Jesus's first disciples did. Our faith confronts us with this decision every single day.

Ernest Shackleton was an amazing captain who led a group of tired men on a miraculous journey through the cold and stormy seas in nothing but a lifeboat against every conceivable odd. The journey was hazardous, but Shackleton was a faithful

commander—not a single life was lost because of his compe-
tency, care, and leadership.

We can endure in the Christian life because we, too, have
a committed, loving, and faithful Savior who understands our
experience of life's storms. As the Bible says, the Captain of our
salvation has been made perfect through what he suffered with
us and for us (see Heb. 2:10).[25] "This is the will of him who sent
me," Jesus said, "that I shall *lose none* of all those he has given me"
(John 6:39). An unshakable sense that we are eternally safe in
God's hands is ultimately what helps us endure those moments
that feel so scary. We may feel lost, but we cannot ever be lost, as
we are forever found in Christ from the foundation of the world.

Can life be excruciatingly tough? Are there seasons of profound confusion and stormy seas that we must brave? Yes, of
course. However, we still cling to Jesus throughout the storms
because we know that Jesus will forever cling to us. We can live
with our questions because, in Christ, we have God's answer.

"Do you also wish to go away?" This is the question that Jesus
asked Peter, and that we are also asked. God give us grace to
answer as Peter did. "Lord, to whom can we go? You have the
words of eternal life."

Discussion Questions

1. Would you describe the Christian life as a "hazardous journey"? Why or why not?
2. When have you found endurance to be most difficult in your
   own faith journey? When have you been most confused?
   How did you work through it?
3. What does vulnerability with God look like? Do you think
   vulnerability is important to endure in the spiritual life?
   Why or why not?

---

25. Please note that the NRSV translates ἀρχηγός as "pioneer," but "captain" also works.

Chapter 15

Freedom

Then Jesus, filled with the power of the Spirit, returned to Galilee, and a report about him spread through all the surrounding country. He began to teach in their synagogues and was praised by everyone. When he came to Nazareth, where he had been brought up, he went to the synagogue on the Sabbath day, as was his custom. He stood up to read, and the scroll of the prophet Isaiah was given to him. He unrolled the scroll and found the place where it was written: "The Spirit of the Lord is upon me, because he has anointed me to bring good news to the poor. He has sent me to proclaim release to the captives and recovery of sight to the blind, to let the oppressed go free, to proclaim the year of the Lord's favor." And he rolled up the scroll, gave it back to the attendant, and sat down. The eyes of all in the synagogue were fixed on him. Then he began to say to them, "Today this scripture has been fulfilled in your hearing." (Luke 4:14–21)

The first year of my priesthood I vividly recall sitting at a coffee shop when I received the following text message: "You are being very inappropriate. I hope your parishioners can't see your Facebook page."

As I sat stunned and pondered how to respond, my phone rang. A friend was calling to express concerns about my Facebook activity. I quickly tried logging onto my account only to find that my password had been changed. I knew immediately that my account had been hacked. My phone rang off the hook for the next three hours as friend after friend berated me with questions about the things I was posting online. "Why did you tell Ben that dogs ate his brother? Why did you tell Christy that Darth Vader was going to kill you? Why are you dating an eighty-seven-year-old man?"

This hacker was clearly having a lot of fun at my expense, but at the time I was not laughing. I felt completely helpless, power-less, and out of control. Someone was holding me captive and wreaking havoc in my personal life. There was nothing I could do about it. I felt like a prisoner.

Having one's social media account hacked isn't a big deal in the grand scheme of things. It only took me a few days to get my account back online and to clean up all the relational messes that my hacker created. However, the panic we feel when confronted with injustice is very real. We hate feeling helpless, powerless, and out of control. These feelings of cap-tivity remind us how the world *should* be, and we feel grief, sadness, and anger at the incongruence between God's dream for the world and the all too real nightmare that character-izes life for far too many people. We think of Hitler, a devas-tating earthquake that kills thousands, the growing refugee crises, political injustice, systemic racism, or gun violence, and we shake our head in bafflement. "That's not right," we say. "Things are supposed to be different. We need to fix that." For a moment we feel empowered, but feelings of powerlessness creep in the moment we realize that we *can't* fix our world. We are held captive by the forces of evil, chance, circumstance, and unjust social structures.

We will understand the hope that Jesus offers our world only if we are in touch with these very real feelings of helplessness. Jesus's first audience was certainly acquainted with such feelings. The Jews in Jesus's day were a conquered people. The Romans ruled over them, and the Jews felt imprisoned by the presence, politics, and paganism of Caesar's regime.

Jews in Jesus's day also felt spiritually captive. They yearned for personal holiness. A verse from Psalm 51 sums it all up: "I was born guilty and I have been a sinner from my mother's womb." Many Jews felt insecure about their relationship with God. Sacrifices were made, rituals observed, and Sabbaths honored, but all the while a deep feeling of disconnect and shame shackled their hearts. They tried to follow God's law perfectly and they failed. Their inability to be God's holy people made them feel like prisoners.

Their feelings of captivity even extended beyond the political and spiritual realms. Jesus's first audience felt like *ecological* captives, too. They believed that the entire creation was imprisoned and that it needed to be set free. When confronted with earthquakes and storms, the scorching heat and bitter cold, and even animals hunting and killing one another, they remembered the prophets' vision of a world where the lion and lamb could play together in a unified and restored world. Paul mentions this harmonized ecology when he says that the creation itself is waiting to be set free from bondage (see Romans 8:19).

Jesus's first audience felt like prisoners, and the essence of their hope was that God would act in a decisive and mighty way to set them free. They could not accept the status quo. There was no Hebrew equivalent of *c'est la vie* or "that's just how the cookie crumbles." They hungered for a better world, and they expected God to create a better world, a world where the cookie *didn't* crumble. This hope for a better world where all people and even creation itself would be set free was the essence of the Jewish faith. They prayed for freedom, expected it, and wrote about it, and they actively waited for God's new world where all were free.

Isaiah, perhaps more than any other prophet, championed their belief that a new world was on its way and that God would anoint a Messiah to set God's people free.

This is an important backdrop if we are to understand Jesus's words: "I have come to let the oppressed go free." This is Jesus's mission statement, his manifesto, his public declaration of who he is and what he came to do. "The Spirit of the Lord is upon me," Jesus announces, "because he has anointed me to bring good news to the poor, to proclaim release to the captives, and to let the oppressed go free."

Jesus knows that he speaks these words to a people who felt imprisoned and who yearned for freedom as they waited for a Messiah. Into their imprisoned reality, and ours, Jesus speaks words of hope: "I have come to set you free. I will set the creation free. I am in control and I will fix things. The Lord has anointed *me* to set the creation free."

Deep down, we know things are supposed to be different. We can all name countless places in our world and in our personal lives where we long for freedom, wholeness, and congruence. In our heart of hearts, we are no different from Jesus's first audience in our hunger for a unified world. We want a world where everyone prospers, where tectonic plates don't shift and cause earthquakes, and where people both know the right thing to do and desire to do it. We hunger for a world that is free.

The good news of the Christian gospel is that God has brought freedom to our world in and through the incarnation, death, and resurrection of Jesus Christ. As Paul writes, "For freedom Christ has set us free" (Gal. 5:1). The miracle and wonder of the Christian faith is that Jesus would willingly become a captive, indeed a death-row inmate, so that you and I could be free.

As I ponder what it means to be a conduit of God's reckless love, I return time and time again to this foundational assertion: we are free in Christ right now. We may continue to experience sin, fear, and death, but we know that the mystery of our faith is that in Christ all things have already been made new. From our time-bound perspective, we certainly wait for the cosmic revelation of that mystery.

A deep heart-knowledge that we are free right now will change how we respond to our feelings of imprisonment and injustice. Indeed, knowledge of our freedom in Christ compels us to respond to injustice as Jesus did, in the most foolish and counterintuitive of ways: by *forgiving* it. I do not mean that we passively accept injustice. I just mean that our first choice, when confronted with our world's pain, is always to forgive the injustice for existing and to affirm our belief that, in Christ, all pain and suffering has already been dealt with.

Jesus is the Anointed One, but in our baptism, we, too, were anointed. A priest took some oil, made the sign of the cross on our head, and marked us as Christ's own forever. The Spirit of the Lord is also upon us, and our great joy is to join Jesus in his mission to bring good news to the poor, to proclaim release to the captives, and to let the oppressed go free.

Do not make the mistake of thinking that the poor and oppressed captive that Jesus wants to free is anyone other than *you*. Only people who know they are free in Christ can bring freedom to other people.

Discussion Questions

1. Where do you see oppression most clearly in our world? In your life? What good news does the gospel offer us in the midst of that oppression?
2. What does the word freedom mean to you? Can you think of anything specific in your life that Christ has set you free from?
3. What does the word anointed mean to you? Do you believe that you are anointed by God? Why or why not?

Chapter 16

Betrayal

Just after daybreak, Jesus stood on the beach; but the disciples did not know that it was Jesus. Jesus said to them, "Children, you have no fish, have you?" They answered him, "No." He said to them, "Cast the net to the right side of the boat, and you will find some." So they cast it, and now they were not able to haul it in because there were so many fish. That disciple whom Jesus loved said to Peter, "It is the Lord!" When Simon Peter heard that it was the Lord, he put on some clothes, for he was naked, and jumped into the lake. But the other disciples came in the boat, dragging the net full of fish, for they were not far from the land, only about a hundred yards off. When they had gone ashore, they saw a charcoal fire there, with fish on it, and bread. Jesus said to them, "Bring some of the fish that you have just caught." So Simon Peter went aboard and hauled the net ashore, full of large fish, a hundred and fifty-three of them; and though there were so many, the net was not torn. Jesus said to them, "Come and have breakfast." Now none of the disciples dared to ask him, "Who are you?" because they knew it was the Lord. Jesus came and took the bread and gave it to them, and did the same with the fish. This was now the third time that Jesus appeared to the disciples after he was raised from the dead. When they had finished breakfast, Jesus said to Simon Peter, "Simon son of John, do you love me more than these?" He said to him, "Yes, Lord; you know that I love you." Jesus said to him, "Feed my lambs." A second time he said to him, "Simon son of John, do you love me?" He said to him, "Yes, Lord; you know that I love you." Jesus said to him, "Tend my sheep." He said to him the third time, "Simon son of John, do you love me?" Peter felt hurt because he said to him the third time, "Do you love me?" And he said to him, "Lord, you know everything; you know that I love you." Jesus said to him, "Feed my sheep." (John 21:4–17)

A few years ago, I was asked to speak to a group of high school students about betrayal. If you are acquainted with the frightening social jungle we call high school, you undoubtedly will understand the relevance of this topic to a group of teens. I began by asking them to list as many famous betrayals as they could. They came up with a wonderfully diverse list, ranging from Brutus's betrayal of Julius Caesar all the way down to Regina George's betrayal of Cady Heron in the classic *Mean Girls*. When I asked for biblical examples of betrayal, I assumed that everyone would cite Judas. Much to my surprise, the person they were most fixated on was Peter. It was Peter, they said, who betrayed Jesus the most precisely because he so vehemently promised that he never would.

John 21 recalls Peter and the risen Jesus's first one-on-one encounter after a hurtful and serious betrayal on Peter's part. Jesus predicted that all his disciples would betray him, but at the time Peter did not believe Jesus and swore with all the passion he could muster: "Even if I must die with you, I will not deny you" (Matt. 26:35). Hours later, as the cock crowed for the third time,

Peter scurried to save his own neck. Jesus, meanwhile, is blood-ied and beaten and will soon be crucified.

Think for a moment about this betrayal. It is tragic enough that Peter lost his Lord and his best friend, but in a sense Peter lost so much more that night—his integrity, his credentials as a leader, and perhaps even his own sense of worth as a human being. Peter didn't just lose his Lord but also the illusion that he was the rock. The weight of his sin came crashing down, and Peter was forced to see that he was not better, holier, or even more faithful to Jesus than the men who drove the nails through Jesus's wrists.

How do you recover from *that* experience?

Very slowly, perhaps as you return to the life you knew before you met Jesus—which is precisely what Peter does. Peter returns to his work as a fisherman. Peter jumps back into his old routine and does what he can to keep the crushing grief at bay.

With one fishing expedition, everything changes for Peter. The setting is just after daybreak, as the night is coming to an end and the sun's light begins to dispel the darkness of the night (pause and ponder the deep theological significance). Seeing Jesus standing on the beach, Peter puts on his clothes and jumps into the water because apparently, he likes to fish in the nude.

As humorous as this scene might sound, the Bible is trying to convey Peter's shame of his betrayal. You may recall the story of Adam and Eve. They betray God's trust by disobeying God's com-mand. Like Peter, they immediately realize that they are naked, they cover themselves, and they hide from God because they are scared and ashamed. This is precisely what Peter does the moment he realizes that he is in the Lord's presence. Feeling the humiliation of his betrayal, Peter covers his nakedness because he does not want to be seen.

Place yourself for a moment in Peter's (soaking wet) sandals. If you were going to meet Jesus for the very first time after betray-ing him in such an egregious way, what would you say? What do you think that Jesus would say to you?

There is a part of us that connects deeply with Peter's story. We so badly want to follow Jesus to the cross and to live as self-sacrificially as he did as we pour out our life in reckless love for others. We want to walk our talk and reflect the truth we profess in how we live. We all have this spiritually zealous part of ourselves that, under certain conditions, will boldly declare with Peter: "Even if I must die with you I will not deny you" (Mark 14:31). However, when push comes to shove, we often run away and save our own necks. Our fear usually wins the spiritual tug of war that is forever happening in our soul and that makes us feel shame. We deeply desire to be faithful to Jesus, but we are only willing to follow him so far and to suffer so much.

This is the tension that runs through the heart of every Christian. We want to be faithful, and we frequently fail to be. We often manage this tension by not letting Jesus get too close. We stay in the boat. We play it safe. We come to church, give some money, take Eucharist, participate in a program, and uphold our status as a "member in good standing," but we never take the risk that Peter did and plunge into the water. We settle for church but never get to know the Lord intimately simply because we feel unworthy for the many ways we know that we betray Jesus.

Where are you in that story?

Peter is a leader; he does not let his sin and shame keep him from jumping out of the boat and going to meet his Lord on the beach. Peter may not be perfect, but he knows that grace and mercy flow from Jesus's presence. This knowledge gives him confidence to go and meet his Lord on the beach and experience the deep healing, restoration, and intimacy that Jesus longs to give all people—even you.

This is why Jesus calls Peter by name. Jesus knows all of us by name. Metaphorically speaking, we clothe ourselves and try to cover our shame so that the Lord does not see us. But the fact remains that Jesus *does see us* and that Jesus loves what he sees. Jesus looks at our uniqueness and sees with crystal clarity the games we play, the hidden hopes and fears, and the longings of our heart. Jesus sees it all—the good, the bad, the ugly—and he calls the real us by name. Jesus sees us, even if we cannot see ourselves. Jesus is not disgusted by what he sees, disappointed by what he sees, or angered by what he sees. Jesus calls each one of us by name and loves us.

Jesus restores Peter by asking him a question. The deeper I go into my own prayer life, the more convinced I become that this is the only question that Jesus ever asks his frail, conflicted, and sinful disciples. That question is not, "Are you sorry?" or "Have you learned from your mistake?" or "What are you doing for my Kingdom?" or "Are you improving spiritually?" The only question Jesus has any interest in asking anyone at any time is this: "Do you love me?"

This question Jesus asks us is very vulnerable in nature. It leaves us with power to say yes or no, to pay attention to Jesus's presence in our life or to ignore Jesus's presence. This question is also deeply intertwined with a second question: do we know how deeply Jesus loves us? What fuels our love for Jesus is a deep heart-knowledge of Jesus's love for us. As the New Testament shares, "We love because he first loved us" (1 John 4:19).

There is no shame in confessing that we routinely betray Jesus. Christians get themselves into a lot of trouble when they disown their lack of faithfulness and, like Peter, insist that they are not capable of denying Jesus. We betray Jesus daily with our thoughts, our desires, and with any action that denies any human being dignity and worth. The theological word for this betrayal is *sin*.

That may sound depressing, but it isn't. The truth is never disappointing because the truth is what sets us free. God's grace abounds all the more in our betrayal. Jesus stands on the beach with open arms beckoning us to jump out of the boat. The night of humiliation has ended, and the light of Christ's grace over-flows our nets.

Our unfaithfulness, at the end of the day, is a small matter to God. Jesus's fidelity to us is always the only thing that matters.

Indeed, it is the very bread we are given to feed Jesus's sheep. The last thing God desires is that a group of self-espoused super-humans go out into the world with their own strength, skills, and bread to feed God's people. That's not mission, but madness. Authentic mission begins when a group of people are honest with themselves about their own sin and, knowing that they betray Jesus daily, still approach him naked to be judged, shaken, undone, and restored by the most piercing of all questions: do you love me?

Discussion Questions

1. Where in your spiritual life do you frequently betray Jesus, or where do your actions consistently fail to align with your values? Do you see this as a "problem"? Why or why not?
2. Have you ever betrayed or been betrayed by another human being? How did that experience impact you, and was forgiveness offered/received?
3. Do you believe Jesus sees the fullness of who you are? If so, does that thought offer you relief or anxiety? Why?

Chapter 17

Waiting

Now a certain man was ill, Lazarus of Bethany, the village of Mary and her sister Martha. Mary was the one who anointed the Lord with perfume and wiped his feet with her hair; her brother Lazarus was ill. So the sisters sent a message to Jesus, "Lord, he whom you love is ill." But when Jesus heard it, he said, "This illness does not lead to death; rather it is for God's glory, so that the Son of God may be glorified through it." Accordingly, though Jesus loved Martha and her sister and Lazarus, after having heard that Lazarus was ill, he stayed two days longer in the place where he was. (John 11:1–6)

When my wife and I moved into our new home after our wedding, my commute to and from work changed. One of the first things I noticed about my new route was a beautiful brick mansion that was under construction and seemingly almost complete. The foundation had been laid and the edifice was built, but the house still needed windows, landscaping, wiring, and inner beautification. As a lover of HGTV, I was very excited to see this house come to completion.

It only took me a few drives home to realize that this project had stalled and its completion would have to wait. Day after day I couldn't help but wonder: will the owner ever return and complete what was started?

Our life sometimes feels like an empty house. It may be beautiful on the outside, structurally sound, and perhaps even situated on the right lot. However, we can also feel stalled at times and painfully incomplete. Every human being longs for completion. When a mass shooting leaves a dozen dead, someone I love is diagnosed with an illness, or I look at my innocent toddler and know that I cannot protect her from suffering, I am reminded that I am waiting for Jesus to complete me. I sometimes wonder what is taking Jesus so long and what work God wants to accomplish in my soul as I wait.

Surely this is how Mary and Martha felt when they sent word to Jesus that Lazarus had fallen ill. They know that Jesus has the power to heal their brother and that Jesus loves Lazarus. They assume that Jesus will drop whatever he is doing, come to Bethany, and cure him at once. But this, of course, is not what Jesus does. In fact, after getting word that Lazarus is terminally ill Jesus stays where he is for another two days. By the time Jesus does arrive, Lazarus has been dead four days. John's Gospel doesn't tell us what takes Jesus so long, but two things emerge with crystal clarity. First, Jesus is not in a hurry. Second, Martha and Mary are powerless to do anything other than wait for Jesus to arrive.

It may sound odd, but I find Jesus's lack of urgency oddly comforting. My problems always feel so important, but from Jesus's point of view our anxiety is totally out of place. Jesus seems to know something that I don't; my spiritual "work" is to wait for Jesus to arrive. I am responsible for the quality of my presence as I wait for Jesus. I couldn't have healed Lazarus myself, or the refugee crises today, if I wanted to. But I can breathe deeply, wait on Jesus, and take appropriate action from this place of active expectancy. No one needs a seminary degree or a grasp of systematic theology to do *that*. All one needs is faith in the trust-worthiness and wisdom of the One upon whom we wait.

We are not just waiting for Jesus to heal our world. We are also waiting for Jesus to heal us. I was seventeen years old when I became intentional about the quality of my relationship with Jesus. I recall being confident that God was getting a great deal having me on God's team. When I first read the Sermon on the Mount and the charge to "Be perfect, as your heavenly Father is perfect," I remember telling Jesus in a time of prayer (and how badly I wish this were a fabrication): "Jesus, I may need a little bit of time, but I think I am almost there."

Twenty years later, I am *not* almost there. I am still waiting for Jesus to complete me. Like Mary and Martha, my spiritual power is found in my powerlessness to do anything other than wait for Jesus to arrive.

American poet Molly Carr very humorously expresses our dependence on God's arrival. When asked about her conversion to Christianity and the difference her newfound faith made in her life, she responded along these lines: "Before I was a Christian, I wanted to kill all of the people on the New York subway. Now that Jesus has entered my life, I just want to kill *some* of the people on the New York subway."[26] Like all of us, Molly Carr is still waiting for completion.

When we lose touch with our need to wait on God, things go badly and turn to violence, whether that is emotional violence or physical violence. Our world's violence is fueled by the conflicting desires of six billion humans and several hundred nations seeking to impose their will upon the world in a vain effort to usher in their "version" of the kingdom of God. In the United States, this "we can complete ourselves" myth plays out in the

---

26. I borrow this illustration from *Law and Gospel: A Theology for Sinners and Saints* (Charlottesville, VA: Mockingbird Ministries, 2015), 62. This quote is a paraphrase of Molly Carr's words and not drawn directly from *Law and Gospel*.

boring, idolatrous, repetitive lie that believes that when we elect the right politician or pass the right legislation and get rid of the "bad guys" we will finally be complete. The problem is that *we* are the "bad guys." We are also the good guys. The whole human drama of good and evil plays out in the depths of every human soul. All we can do is wait for God to separate the good from the bad (see Matthew 13:29–30).

The brokenness and pain in your body, mind, family, community, and in our world really is not a problem from God's vantage point. Despite the many ways that humanity tries to sabotage God's work, God will bring to completion our lives and our world. This is what "waiting" for Jesus is all about. God desires that we live and feel the tension of our incompleteness rather than trying to resolve it on our own. One can argue that this willingness to feel incomplete *together* is the very essence of faith and the birthplace of all creativity, joy, community, and even justice.

What is Christian community if not a group of people who are courageous enough to live in the tension of being incomplete together? Our joy is found in supporting one another and being supported in that fragile and vulnerable place of waiting for God to finish what God started. This communal posture whereby we actively wait for God together is deeply attractive to the world. Deep down, people know that most of the world's ills stem from our hasty and shortsighted attempts to solve problems. We solve one problem only to create two more. Look deeply at your life and our world and you will see that this is so.

Ultimately, what makes the church unique is not that we are complete and everyone else is incomplete. What makes the church unique is we tell the truth about our need for completion as we proclaim our belief that completion will come when Christ returns. In our Eucharistic prayer we proclaim, "Christ has died. Christ has risen. Christ will come again" (BCP, 363). This is the most countercultural thing we say. We believe that the owner will return and complete what was started and that God's work of completion is already underway, albeit in a dark, hidden, and mysterious way.

After two years of driving by this stalled house, I finally saw a team of workers in front of that red brick home. They were back at work painting the trim, landscaping, and beautifying the insides. The owner returned and completed the good work he started.

Paul writes: "I am confident of this, that the one who began a good work among you will bring it to completion by the day of Christ Jesus" (Phil. 1:6). Do you believe that he who began a very good work in your life will bring it to completion in God's own time and in God's own way? If so, how might that belief change the quality of your life right now?

Discussion Questions

1. Where in your life are you waiting for completion? Do you see any spiritual value in this posture of "waiting?" If so, what?
2. Do you see any difference between actively waiting for God and passive inaction? What connection might exist between a posture of active waiting and justice?
3. Newton writes, the "whole human drama lives in the depths of every human soul. All we can do is wait for God to separate the good from the bad." Do you agree? Why or why not?

Chapter 18

Power

Pilate, wanting to release Jesus, addressed them again; but they kept shouting, "Crucify, crucify him!" A third time he said to them, "Why, what evil has he done? I have found in him no ground for the sentence of death; I will therefore have him flogged and then release him." But they kept urgently demanding with loud shouts that he should be crucified; and their voices prevailed. So Pilate gave his verdict that their demand should be granted. (Luke 23:20–24)

What do you want to be when you grow up? I was asked this question countless times as a child and my answer was always the same: a king. I took the whole "you can do whatever you want in life" advice a little too seriously. I was hungry for power, and I really did want to be a king. I loved the idea of being in charge. "Can I be in charge until you get back?" This is the question I relentlessly asked my parents each time they went to the grocery store or even to the bathroom. "No," they said. "The babysitter is in charge. Your older sister is in charge. The dog is in charge." I hated all those answers because *I* so badly wanted to be in charge.

An aspiring king never forgets his first opportunity to rule. It was junior high, and I was alone with my brother for a few hours after school each day. There was a list of chores that we were responsible for completing and, because I was in charge, the division of labor was quite simple. My younger brother did all the work, and I would supervise. I was a harsh taskmaster. I would bark orders, enforce penalties, and carry around a clipboard, the sign of my authority. I thought the arrangement worked quite well, but my brother complained, a sitter was hired, and I was dethroned. I wasn't a very good king.

Christianity is the story of the world's true king. In Jesus, we believe that the world's long-awaited king has arrived, and that leaves us with some questions. Do we understand the true nature of power? Do we desire to adopt Jesus's model of being "in charge"?

No one really understood Jesus's revolutionary rule, at least not at first. In Luke 23, Jesus is sentenced to die by way of crucifixion. He is mocked, taunted, and shamed. It has been only one week since his triumphal entry into Jerusalem, where Jesus was met as a king with shouts of joy and great expectation. The people were excited because they believed that in Jesus their long-awaited king had finally arrived. People even spread their cloaks on the road to honor Jesus as he passed by. "Hosanna!" they shouted at the top of their lungs. "Blessed is the coming kingdom of our ancestor David!" However, only one week later the shouts have dramatically shifted from "Hosanna, hosanna" to "Crucify him, crucify him!" Jesus was clearly not the sort of king the people were expecting.

You will recall, the Jewish people had been under foreign oppression for centuries and they hungered for freedom. They desperately wanted a king to wipe away the foreign oppressors and restore harmony to their land. Some people expected a military king, while others expected a rabbinic figure. People's expectations may have differed, but they shared one common thread: everyone expected a king who would use earthly power to usher in God's new age.

The beauty of the Christian story is that somewhere amidst that mess of swirling expectations and desires, the true King of creation entered our world. To paraphrase C.S. Lewis, the Author of the play stepped onto the stage and no one recognized him. As the Gospel puts it, "He came unto his own and his own did not receive him" (John 1:11). No one expected a young carpenter to emerge from an insignificant corner of the Roman Empire to announce that in and through his presence and ministry the kingdom of God had finally arrived. This is the irony of the gospel. In a world where all were expecting a king, the true King stepped onto the scene and, aside from a few misfits and peasants, no one even noticed.

Have *we* noticed?

It is all too easy to say that we believe that Jesus is the King of the world and to continue to live as if we are the ones in charge. We love being in the driver's seat. We instinctually try to control our own life and manipulate other people's lives and, suffice it to say, we experience more than our fair share of head-on collisions.

There is a wonderful line in the Book of Common Prayer that speaks to our take-charge impulse. "You made us the rulers of creation. But we turned against you, and betrayed your trust; and we turned against one another" (BCP, 370). Translation: we continually choose power over love. Far too often, our life becomes a series of passive-aggressive moves and countermoves to defend our petty kingdoms. This desire for power has blinded us, and we have lost the ability to see people as they really are— children of God made in the image of Christ, the true King of the world.

The good news of the gospel is that Jesus Christ is King and that Jesus died to restore our broken world, our broken relationships, and our broken heart. The cross shows us that true power is found in a willingness to be powerless for the sake of the beloved. Power is not about taking and becoming more, but about emptying ourselves and becoming less.

Jesus is not the sort of king that anyone could expect or might naturally want. Jesus is not a harsh taskmaster. He does not punish the bad guys but dies for them. The crown he chooses is not made of gold but thorns. When Jesus marched into Jerusalem, he did so not on a stallion or warhorse but on a donkey—a symbolic way of saying God was a Prince of Peace, not a warmongering king (see Zechariah 9:9). Above all, Jesus's mission was not to overthrow Rome or any power "outside" of us. The war Jesus waged was on sin, and Jesus defeated that enemy in his flesh by taking the form of a slave and dying on a cross.

We assume that in taking the form of a slave, Jesus was wearing a costume and disguising the All-Powerful and Mighty God. But here is the scandal of the gospel: Christ the King does not disguise God's true nature, but reveals it. God is the infinite servant, the humblest person in the entire universe. Jesus did not become a slave despite his divine nature, but rather precisely because of that nature. This is what it means for God to be King. The true King recklessly empties himself of all power and rights, dying for the sake of the beloved.

Jesus is a king who washes his disciples' feet and who feels equally at home with prostitutes and lepers as much as with the righteous and the respected. Jesus is the king whose chief delight is to show mercy. Jesus is the king who willingly submitted to a violent death on a Roman cross and then begged his Father to forgive the very people who arranged for that death. Above all, Jesus is the king whose power is revealed not in the breaking of bones but in the breaking of bread. This is the mystery of our faith.

Now an adult, I still want to be a king. I am just learning that the type of king that God is shaping me into is not what I ever expected. One does not grow up and become king. One *grows down* into kinghood. The King I serve and the King who serves me is not seated on a throne, but nailed to a cross. He has launched a revolution of reckless love and turned the world's notion of power and kingship upside down, and in doing so God invites us to reign with him as we empty ourselves to bless the world.

Discussion Questions

1. In what way did Jesus fail to meet people's expectations? In what ways does Jesus fail to meet your expectations?
2. What is the difference between worldly power and the power that Jesus exhibits on the cross? Is a Christian ever permitted to use "worldly power" for a noble end? Why or why not?
3. Where in your life does your desire to "be in charge" manifest most clearly? Does that impulse ever cause you and others pain?

Chapter 19

Hope

After the sabbath, as the first day of the week was dawning, Mary Magdalene and the other Mary went to see the tomb. And suddenly there was a great earthquake; for an angel of the Lord, descending from heaven, came and rolled back the stone and sat on it. His appearance was like lightning, and his clothing white as snow. For fear of him the guards shook and became like dead men. But the angel said to the women, "Do not be afraid; I know that you are looking for Jesus who was crucified. He is not here; for he has been raised, as he said. Come, see the place where he lay. Then go quickly and tell his disciples, 'He has been raised from the dead, and indeed he is going ahead of you to Galilee; there you will see him.' This is my message for you." So they left the tomb quickly with fear and great joy, and ran to tell his disciples. Suddenly Jesus met them and said, "Greetings!" And they came to him, took hold of his feet, and worshipped him. Then Jesus said to them, "Do not be afraid; go and tell my brothers to go to Galilee; there they will see me." (Matt. 28:1–10)

I recently noticed a spider web in our garage. I am not a huge fan of spiders; when I see a spider, I make my wife kill it. However, there was no spider in this web and so, in a very virile way, I took a broomstick, closed my eyes, and began swinging. I felt relief when the web crumbled to the ground in fragments, and I recall thinking, "that was that."

The next day I saw that the spider had replaced the web that I broke. This time her web was bigger, more complex, and even more beautiful than before. The spider was a formidable foe, and I could not help but deeply admire her creativity and resiliency. But I quickly put my warm feelings aside and used a can of military-grade wasp spray to reduce version 2.0 of this web to a few meager strands. This time I *knew* "that was that."

I was wrong again. When I returned home, I was shocked to see that those very strands formed the basis of a new web so impressive and intricate that I was speechless in the face of its beauty. Both times I thought I was breaking the web and putting an end to its life, but my destructive actions were accounted for and factored into a larger process whereby the spider made her web increasingly beautiful. When I did my absolute worst, the spider used it to create her absolute best—a creation more beautiful than had her web never been broken.

Roughly two thousand years ago, the world did its absolute worst by crucifying the Son of God, the world's true King. The hope of God's kingdom arriving once and for all was torn to shreds when Jesus died. Think about the spiritual and psychological state of the two Marys in the story of the visit to the tomb. I imagine they felt defeated, lost, and deeply afraid. The world had done its absolute worst to them and to their leader. The two Marys left everything to follow Jesus. They witnessed this man kiss lepers, cure the sick, give power to the marginalized and hope to the hopeless, but now he has been killed and thrown out like trash. As they walk to the tomb on that first Easter morn, the web of their soul is broken.

We all know something of their defeat and their fear. Even after Jesus's resurrection from the dead, very little in the appearance of our world changed. The Romans continued to crucify people, nations continued to war, and plagues continued to ravage villages. This realization that God allows evil to exist is what makes faith seemingly impossible for so many people. God allows the web of creation, the web of our soul, and the web of our families to be knocked down by the broom of our sin, our selfishness, and our sickness. When a young child dies of cancer, when the only cure we can imagine for war is war, or when we cannot save someone we love, we feel the world doing its worst. We also feel scared, guilty, and powerless because *we* are that world. We want to be part of the solution, but the problem resides deep within us. As Ernest Hemingway purportedly said, eventually "Life breaks everyone."

A healthy acknowledgment of our defeat, our fear, and our powerlessness to transform the world is always the context in which true and lasting hope is experienced. An authentic spirituality will not lose touch with our need for rescue. Only from a place of need can we hear the words of the angel spoken to the Marys. "I know you came to this tomb looking for a dead person. However, this man you love and who loves you, this man you hoped would heal our world and your life, he is not here and he is certainly not dead. Jesus has risen" (see Matt. 28:5–6).

I recently heard a story about a convert to Christianity. His friends were curious about why he decided to become a Christian. "All religions," they rightly pointed out, "have deep wisdom to offer about life and human existence. Why Jesus?" I thought his answer was clever. "Suppose you are going down a road that forks in two different directions and you do not know which way to go. At the fork are two men, one dead and the other alive. Which man would *you* ask for directions?"

Christian hope is deeply rooted in a belief that our Lord, Savior, teacher, king, and friend Jesus Christ is alive. When we did our absolute worst by crucifying the Word made flesh, God used our worst, accounted for it, and factored it in so that God might give the world the ultimate gift: raising Jesus Christ from the dead.

I confess that I am a sucker for self-help books. I am always looking for a tip or trick to calm my nerves and center my being. However, I know that my hope as a Christian cannot rest on anything I do. My ultimate trust is not in a system, practice, or technique, but rather in a person who I believe is alive. Christian hope has nothing to do with faith in progress, the evolution of human consciousness, the power of the human spirit, or how we might overcome. The bedrock of our hope is that *God has overcome* every sin, mistake, accident, and defeat. God has overcome the many ways the web of our soul has been torn, by raising Jesus Christ from the dead.

I recently found myself rummaging through old photos and pictures of my past. I marveled that who I was then seems so different from who I am now, and I began to think how neat it would be if I could see a picture of my future. Then, in a moment of absolute clarity, I realized that I do have that picture. In Jesus Christ risen from the dead, God gives us a picture of our future self in Christ. We are raised, our bodies are healed, and we are utterly alive.

We may experience the suffering of our world as deeply confusing, scary, and meaningless. However, God sees the whole human drama differently, as already resolved in Christ. In the same way that the spider took the places where I broke her web to reweave it into something more beautiful than before, the resurrection of Jesus Christ from the dead is our assurance that this is what God intends to do with our life.

How has life broken *you?*

Ponder the addiction, the fear, the shame, the regret, the pain, the disease, the unresolved relationship, or the career that never took off. Our deep hope and belief is that, from these meager strands, God is rewriting our story in such a way that our future self is more beautiful, more joyful, and more alive than had the web of our soul never been torn in the first place. This is our assurance, the meaning behind the angel sitting on the stone that formerly had been used to cover Jesus's dead body. The angel is flaunting the power of God to bring good out of evil and new life out of death.

Hope is not to be confused with optimism, a belief that things will never go wrong. Things will eventually go wrong for most of us. Hope is a belief that all wrongness has forever been nailed to Jesus's cross and that in his resurrection God forever makes it right. The resurrection of Jesus from the dead exposes our fear, our anxiety, and our pain for what it truly is: empty as the tomb on that first Easter morning.

I smile when I think of Pontius Pilate getting the news on that first Good Friday that Jesus was dead. Pilate had mixed feelings about executing Jesus. However, Jesus was not the first man that Pilate crucified and Jesus would not be the last. I imagine that Pilate shrugged his shoulders and poured a cocktail, thinking "that was that."

That was *not* that.

If the resurrection of the Son of God means anything, with God that is *never* that. Never can that sin, that mistake, that death, that tragedy, that loneliness, that confusion, and that unique way the web of your soul has been torn separate you from God's reckless love. That is never that. The web of your soul is being rewoven even now in Jesus Christ.

Gaze no more at the tomb where your fear, anxiety, and despair all live. Jesus is not there, for he has risen. Jesus is alive, and because Jesus lives so do you.

Discussion Questions

1. What does the word hope mean to you? Is hope different from optimism? Why or why not?

2. Is your faith challenged by the evil that exists in our world? Do you believe that God "allows" evil and even uses evil for good? Why or why not?
3. What does Jesus's "resurrection" mean to you personally? What does it mean to believe in the Resurrection?

Chapter 20

Gift

Six days before the Passover Jesus came to Bethany, the home of Lazarus, whom he had raised from the dead. There they gave a dinner for him. Martha served, and Lazarus was one of those at the table with him. Mary took a pound of costly perfume made of pure nard, anointed Jesus's feet, and wiped them with her hair. The house was filled with the fragrance of the perfume. But Judas Iscariot, one of his disciples (the one who was about to betray him), said, "Why was this perfume not sold for three hundred denarii and the money given to the poor?" (He said this not because he cared about the poor, but because he was a thief; he kept the common purse and used to steal what was put into it.) Jesus said, "Leave her alone. She bought it so that she might keep it for the day of my burial. You always have the poor with you, but you do not always have me." (John 12:1–8)

My favorite show on television is *The Big Bang Theory*, a sitcom about a bunch of nerdy physicists and their neighbor, an actress by the name of Penny. My favorite character on the show is Dr. Sheldon Cooper, a genius with far too many eccentricities to name.

Sheldon's finest quirk is the way he relates to gifts. As a scientist, Sheldon is efficient, logical, and calculated. He always keeps the relational score, which means that Sheldon experiences every gift as an obligation. His machinelike brain can't compute the idea that one can give freely with no expectation of reciprocity. A recurring and deeply comedic scenario has Sheldon receiving a gift and then going into an anxious panic because Sheldon believes he is now in the gift-giver's debt. To balance the relational score, Sheldon responds to gifts with utter efficiency.

On one occasion, his friend Howard gives Sheldon a gift that he values at eight dollars. Sheldon quickly pulls out his wallet, gives Howard a ten-dollar bill, and politely asks for two dollars in change. Sheldon turned the gift into a transaction, rebalancing the relational score to ensure that no one was indebted to anyone else.

The humor of these scenes is exceeded only by their brilliance in revealing how deeply uncomfortable we can be with receiving a gift. For instance, your neighbors invite you to their home for dinner for the second time and you have never had them over once. What is your first thought? "We really need to have the Smiths over for dinner." Or consider the example of an expectant mother awaiting her first child. She's bloated, exhausted, and the nursery isn't put together yet. If there were ever a time to just "receive," this would be it. However, there is real internal and external pressure to write a thoughtful, handwritten note for each gift. This pressure exists because we all keep relational score. We know what we take in, and we know what we give. When the scale is not balanced, we get fidgety. We're efficient, logical, and calculated. These are the values that we bring to life and that life brings to us.

At the beginning of the twelfth chapter of John, Jesus and his friends are celebrating something amazing: Jesus has raised Lazarus from the dead. Viewed through the lens of our cultural milieu, I can't help but think Lazarus, upon receiving such a gift, begins thinking: "Jesus raised me from the dead. There is no way I can match that. But the least I can do is have the guy over for falafel."

During the meal, Mary takes a pound of costly perfume and pours the oil on Jesus's feet.[27] This oil costs three hundred denarii, the equivalent of one man's annual salary. Judas gets sick to his stomach because Mary's gift is so inefficient. She could have sold the perfume and used the money to feed a lot of hungry people. Why would Mary just waste it all on Jesus's feet?

There is a large part of us that agrees with Judas. We see a world filled with hungry people. Some hoard much more than they need, whereas most survive, or don't, on much less than they need. It is only natural to want more balance in our world, more equality. The sheer lavishness of taking all one has and wasting it on a foot triggers our inner Sheldon Cooper. We do the math, and the numbers just don't add up.

Social scientists observe that when a technology fully enters a culture, the values of that technology infuse the culture and slowly replace previously held values. What is the mother of all values for machines and technology? *Efficiency.* The New Testament never holds up efficiency as the fruit of the Spirit, and yet I observe that our drive to be efficient, and our corresponding fear of being inefficient, is greater than it has ever been.

Mary's inefficient, illogical, and uncalculated act of love reveals my need for repentance. The reckless love of God in Jesus Christ is not efficient, calculated, logical, or deserved. Holy Scripture calls God's love sheer foolishness. God's love is reckless, prodigal, lavish, and foolish. It is the love of a sower who sows seed not just in the good soil where there is a clear return on investment, but also on the path where the birds will eat it

---

27. You might be wondering: is this the same Mary we saw in chapter nineteen at the empty tomb? Between Mary, Jesus's mother; Mary, mother of James and Joses; Mary of Clopas; Mary of Bethany; and Mary Magdalene, I can't keep up. Keeping track of the different Marys is like a "Who's on first" joke. Good luck keeping it all straight!

and among thorns where it will no doubt get choked. God's math never adds up because the relational score is never balanced, *by design*. The reckless love of God spends all one has on a foot.

Something within my heart resists this love and finds it utterly baffling. If I were the rector of a church and Mary applied for a job, I can say with absolute certainty that I'd pass in favor of a candidate more responsible in stewarding her time and energy. Yet, the gospel gives me permission to be more wasteful with the gift of my time, attention, energy, and money. God's love frees me to honor, value, and celebrate the people like Mary with whom I live and work.

Maybe you are a Mary, and you struggle to find your place and value in a culture where efficiency is king. I hope you see in Mary's lavish gesture overwhelming validation of who God made you to be. I cannot tell you how badly the Church and the world need you to be *you*.

The ultimate significance of Mary's act, however, is not that it teaches us to be more lavish with our love. We are characters in the story quoted above, but I don't think we are Mary. Very few of us have a capacity to be as reckless with our love as she was with hers, at least not all the time. I don't think we are Judas, either. We are not so concerned with efficiency that we stand ready at any moment to ruin the party. Some commentators suggest that we are Lazarus, people who have been raised from the dead and who sit at table with Jesus as his friends. This is true theologically, but also a predictable interpretation of the story. When the scripture becomes predictable, that's when I put it down.

If we are not Mary, Judas, or Lazarus, then who are we? Where do we find ourselves in this passage? Ponder that question for a moment and then turn the page slowly. The answer to this question is the very meaning behind this book.

We are Jesus's feet.
The very costly gift is Jesus, himself: wasted, poured out, and utterly dumped into every crevice of creation to make it holy,

redeemed, and beautified. Jesus is the seed of God's reckless love sown into every ounce of creation. We are Jesus's feet, the recipients of God's most lavish gift—the inefficient, illogical, and uncalculated love of God broken and perpetually poured into all our life, both good soil and thorns.

God gives freely, continually, and lavishly out of God's abundance every moment of every day. God gives and gives and gives with no expectation of reciprocity, which makes zero sense to our logical minds.

Does God's reckless love make sense? Not at all. But there is no need to understand, only the need to receive the gift so that our lives start to make *less sense* to the world.

Discussion Questions

1. When you receive a gift, do you feel the need to reciprocate? If so, how might that instinct to reciprocate show up in your relationship with God?
2. Judas was angry that Mary wasted something so valuable on Jesus's foot. Is there a part of you that understands his anger? What would you have done with the costly perfume?
3. Do you believe that God wants us to be efficient with our time and energy? Why or why not?

SCRIPTURE INDEX